John Gloster

WELCOME

Coign and Woking Baptist

CHURCH STORY

WELCOME

Coign and Woking Baptist

CHURCH STORY

Published by John Gloster
Scillonia Cottage, Manor Road, Horsell GU21 4RY

First Edition, Dec 2018
Book production, cover photo and design by Tony Lyttle
Printed by Amazon

ISBN: 978-1-7307-9632-6

About the author

John Gloster is retired from his job as a research scientist with the Met Office. Married to Gill, they have three grownup children and six grandchildren. From childhood, he has attended the church where his father, Leslie Gloster, was Church Treasurer for many years and a Church Elder. His great-grandfather, Henry William Gloster, was one of the original eight members who formed Woking Baptist Church in 1879.

John Gloster

To my wife, Gill, without whose help and encourage-ment this book would not have been written. More than that, for her love and support for more than forty years.

WELCOME

Coign and Woking Baptist

CHURCH STORY

Written and compiled by

JOHN GLOSTER

All profits to Welcome Church, Woking

FOREWORD
by Steve Petch

It has often been said that history is written by the victors. Of course, those who survived to relate their version of events would naturally paint the past in a way that would portray themselves in the most favourable light.

When it comes to the history of God's people in the Bible, God gives no such special treatment. The great heroes of the faith had their lives recorded for us warts and all; their successes and their failures standing cheek to cheek.

Abraham - lying that his wife was only his sister to save his own skin; Sarah - laughing in utter disbelief at God's promises; Moses - committing murder and trying to hide it in the sand; David - cheating on his wife and then arranging the murder of a faithful friend to cover it up; Mary - declaring her son Jesus was out of his mind; Peter - denying Jesus and running away in fear; Paul - stirring up trouble everywhere he went.

These stories help us to realise that the heroes of our faith were normal people, just like us. Human, fallible, weak … and redeemed by God's grace; all of them were sinners who God declared righteous by faith.

All through history these are the type of people who God has used to build His church and advance His Kingdom, and it's no different in the history of our own Church. It has been built over many decades by fallible people who had their own foibles, their own challenges, their own preferences and their own temptations, arguments, sins and failings to deal with. John Gloster has captured this reality brilliantly in the two volumes of our Church's history that he has written, and this second volume brings us right up to date.

Let me encourage you to read them through - both of them. Some parts will make you laugh, some may make you shake your head in disbelief; some parts will educate you, some may make you wonder what on earth they were thinking; some parts will thrill you and some may inspire you to ask, "What will God do in our day?" One thing is clear however: throughout our history God has been faithful. Jesus is building his Church, just as He promised.

I've been the Lead Pastor here for one year now, and it's been a lot of fun, albeit not without its challenges. I'm very aware that we are 'standing on the shoulders of giants' as we try to follow the call of God in our own day. We recently changed our name to **Welcome Church** … and what will the next generation make of that? Perhaps they will shake their heads at us in their turn, but just maybe we can do something together to inspire them and give them some higher ground to stand on as they take things forward into the future.

For my part, I love God's Church. I've given my life to planting churches and helping them grow. I'm compelled by God's call on my life to teach and feed and lead God's sheep with grace; I can't be content doing anything else. It's a privilege to be called to this Church, but reading this history is a timely reminder that we are each here for a short while, as though we are carrying the baton in a relay race, or running with the Olympic torch.. The time will come to pass the baton on to the next runner, and my prayer is that it will be passed on well and in a good condition - the flame burning bright.

And of course, this history has once again been written by the victors, since every person who contributed to it is in Christ and belongs to Him. And as the Apostle Paul wrote, ***"In all these things we are more than conquerors through him who loved us***. *For I am convinced that neither death nor life, neither angels nor demons, neither the present nor the future, nor any powers, neither height nor depth, nor anything else in all creation, will be able to separate us from the love of God that is ours in Christ Jesus our Lord." (Romans 8 v 37-39)*

What a joy to be part of God's people and to express that faith through belonging to this wonderful and faithful local Church.

Steve Petch
Lead Pastor, Welcome Church
September 2018

ACKNOWLEDGEMENTS

I wish to than many people who have made this book possible including all the contributors to the text, itself: Brian Bonnington, Eddie Bower, Heather Britt, Bryan Cross, Chas Davis, Olive Davis, Janet Deavin, Mike Deavin, David Dennington, David Field, Malcolm Kayes, Christine Leong, Tony Lyttle, David Maskell, James Mellor, Ron Newman, Edie Nunn, Pippa Osborne, Geoff Owers, Steve Petch, Alice Potter, Alan Sussex, Chris Young and the Woking News and Mail. I would like to thank, also, the families of those whose loved ones have contributed to this book and who have since gone to be with their beloved Lord. Their names live on.

And finally, I want to acknowledge the invaluable help of Gill Gloster, Christine Leong, Anita Lyttle and Alice Potter who painstakingly proof-read the manuscript; Max Nurney, for the Welcome Centre photo; and Tony Lyttle for all his hard work on the book production, both text and cover.

If anyone mentioned in the text would prefer their name to be omitted, it will be deleted in subsequent editions.

TABLE OF CONTENTS

CHAPTER **Page**

Great is the Lord and most worthy of praise; His greatness no-one can fathom. One generation will commend your works to another, they will tell of Your mighty acts. (Psalm 145:3-4)

CHAPTER 1

INTRODUCTION

This is the "Welcome Church Story" which is the history of Woking Baptist and The Coign Church from its early days until now. With a few friends I have tried to capture some of the history of our Church that I hope you will enjoy reading.

The events described in this book primarily relate to the times when the Church was led by Rev. Philip Jones, Rev. H G Owen (Harold or Pastor as he was known) and Malcolm Kayes.

The book has been written for six reasons:

- to document some of our rich heritage which, if not recorded, will soon be forgotten and relegated to the mysteries of time. This point has been emphasised by the fact that since I started compiling the book a few years ago, several of the contributors have died and are now with their Heavenly Father.

- to pass some of our roots on to the next generation as we are encouraged to do in the Old Testament. David wrote a psalm of praise which includes the following, "Great is the Lord and most worthy of praise, His greatness no-one can fathom. One generation will commend your works to another, they will tell of Your mighty acts" Psalm 145 v 3 and 4.

- for those with an enquiring mind about our heritage. Steve Petch, Lead Elder at Welcome Church, has encouraged me to record some of the past events to help current Church members come to understand how we have got to where we are today. An example which comes to mind is the emphasis on the work of the Holy Spirit. Has it always been this way, or did something happen to change the Church from being a lively evangelical Church to a Church where the Holy Spirit plays much more of a central role?

- in “A Church on the move – the history of The Coign Church 1879 to 1999 (2009)” I presented a chronological account of the history of the Church. It was recognised at that time that, whilst this format has its merits, there is so much more to tell about life in the Church than a series of facts extracted from Annual, Quarterly and Special Church meeting records and minutes. Church life is about God interacting with many individuals, and each has a unique insight into events as they unfold and their own part to play in the onward move of the Church.

- an account of events involving hundreds of Church members cannot be fully recorded by any single individual as he or she only sees things from one angle. The situation is made more complex as the Holy Spirit doesn’t work the same way in everybody's lives. Also, whilst some of the major events will be observed by many, often some of the most significant ones occur to an individual and are only known to a very limited number of people. Consequently, to try and paint as accurate a picture as possible, I invited a number of people who experienced the events first hand to put pen to paper (or should I say fingers to keyboard) to record their memories. I have taken their input and endeavoured to compile an accurate account of some of the major events.

- I have been actively encouraged to document the events of the past by those who experienced these events first hand and who wish to record their thanks to God for living through both exciting and sometimes more challenging times.

Following a scene-setting chapter we look at a range of issues, ranging from the outpouring of the Holy Spirit to Church accommodation, and various other topics in between. There are many other events which could have been included but unfortunately time has run out. I am sure that I have missed out some important aspects of Church life. If so, please write them down and send them to me and I will see if they can be fitted into a future edition.

The authors don't claim infallibility and would welcome receiving any corrections or amendments. Where possible, permission to quote names has been sought. Hopefully where this has not been possible forgiveness may be granted.

CHAPTER 2

SETTING THE SCENE

The Church was born in September 1879 with eight members, one of which was my Great-Grandad, as a Branch Mission Station under the care of Addlestone Baptist Church. Yes, Church planting has been around for many years. Records indicate that the first meetings were held on a Thursday evening in a house in Goldsworth Road, not that far from the site of the Welcome Centre in 2018. Forty people attended the first meeting not bad for a house group!

Up until the late 1960's the Church was served faithfully by fourteen "full time" Pastors who were assisted by Elders, Deacons and countless volunteers. From the first Pastor,

Rev. Edward Tarbox, until the appointment of Rev. Harold Owen, the spiritual responsibility of the Church was delegated to the Pastor by the Church membership, with other major matters decided upon by Church members at Quarterly, Special or Annual General Meetings chaired by the Pastor. Of those present in the 1960's, who could not forget voting on matters such as the colour of the curtains or the number of communion cups to order? This governance subsequently changed, but more about this later.

Attendance at Church services has fluctuated over the years, but overall there has been a steady increase. Precise numbers of active Church membership are hard to define. For example, at the start of 1899 there were 96 members but only 69 at the end; one of the reasons behind the reduction in numbers was due to a strict analysis of attendance. By 1913, 133 were active communicant members with an additional 30 honorary members. In 1959 it is recorded that 65 members attended the meeting at which Philip Jones was invited to become Pastor (90% in favour). When Harold Owen was invited to become Pastor

107 members attended a Special Church Meeting (92% in favour). When Malcolm Kayes was subsequently invited to become Pastor a total of 244 members attended (85% in favour).

The Church has met together in five main premises. With the exception of a ten-month period, all of the premises have been within several hundred metres of the current site in Church Street West. But let's go back to the early days of the Church. After meeting for a short while in a house in Goldsworth Road, a temporary site was purchased and a building erected close by. Eventually a more permanent Chapel, described at the time in *Baptist Churches in Surrey* (1909) as "a pretty and convenient chapel" was opened in 1886. During the following years Church membership continued to expand and additional properties adjoining the existing building was used to accommodate Church activities. The story sounds so very similar to the situation both in the period covered in this book and in 2018. Problems with space continued until a larger building was constructed in 1924, within a stone's throw of the old Church, with the new building being located in Percy Street (now Victoria Way). Finally, as far as the records go, and for similar reasons as previous moves, the Church moved to its present site, which was named The Coign, on the corner of Church Street West on 8 October 1977. Yet again problems with space arose, and two Sunday services were held at the HG Wells rooms in Woking town centre. After much work and heartache plans for an exciting new build were prepared, submitted and approved by the Woking Borough Council, but more of that later on in the book.

CHAPTER 3

FOUNDATIONS

There are many aspects of Church life which we could examine in detail, but let us concentrate on some key aspects - our beliefs, prayer, praise, worship and evangelism both in the UK and abroad. Let's briefly look at each one.

3.1 Our Beliefs

From the first minister, the Rev. E W Tarbox, right through to the present day, the authority of the Bible and fundamental Christian doctrine has played a pivotal role in Church life. Whether it is through preaching from the front, Church activities, or related to specific events; a belief in the Bible as God's word for His people and assent to its main doctrines have been key to Church life. Let me illustrate this through two very different events - firstly, when a change in leadership was required, and secondly, when a difficult decision had to be made concerning a key doctrine contained in the Bible.

Those familiar with job searching and the selection process know that a good employer will compile a list of essential criteria that applicants must fulfil. It is no different when a new leader of the Church is required. For example, in 1911 when the Church was looking for a new leader three tests for the appointment were agreed by members:

- Does he hold the great essential truths of Christianity?
- Does he have a gift of presenting the truth?
- Does he help members engage more perfectly in the work to which God has called us?

In 1945 Church records identify the following selection criteria "a faithful Christian witness in the town, a soul winner and soul builder".

John Gloster

After the departure of Philip Jones on 31 December 1965 the search for a new Pastor/leader started. Following a period of over a year Gilbert Simmons, one of the elder statesmen on the Diaconate, reported that he had heard of a "good man" in Reading at Carey Street Baptist Church. Conversions were taking place, students were attending in good numbers and the Holy Spirit was active in the lives of the people and the life of the church. Consequently, he was invited to preach on two occasions. On both occasions he was well received, and he was then asked to meet the Deacons. Alan Sussex, a member of the Diaconate, was asked by Malcolm Simpson the then Church Secretary to open the discussions with this man, whose name was Harold Owen. Alan records that, "I started by asking Harold for his view on scripture and its position in the life and governance of the Church. As those of you who remember him can imagine, he gave unequivocal answers that scripture was the Word of God, fully trustworthy, divinely inspired and our supreme authority in all matters related to our faith and conduct. The rest of the meeting flowed well, and soon after that a proposal was put to the Church that he be invited to the Pastorate. This was gladly agreed by the Church and Harold was inducted in June 1967. On reflection, I often think back to that moment when I asked his opening question. It reminds me of the saying, "Ask a silly question and......." but I didn't get a silly answer. It was the answer we were looking for and his love of and knowledge of the scriptures was the hallmark of his ministry".

Over the years there have been numerous difficult decisions for Church leaders and members to make. Some of these involved moving ahead with new building projects even when there were insufficient funds in the accounts, others had a more spiritual dimension and many required dealing in love with individual Church members. During Harold's ministry the Church was faced with a very difficult decision concerning the matter of the central doctrine of the "deity of Christ". In May 1971 Malcolm Simpson, the Church Secretary, informed members that the Church had sent a letter to the Baptist Union concerning the "Deity of Christ" – a senior representative of the Baptist Union had addressed the Baptist Union Conference saying that he could not hold the view that Jesus was both God and man.

An unsatisfactory response was received and so the issue was discussed again by the Church leaders. They decided not to take any further action until the Baptist Union Council had met in November. Regrettably after further discussion, soul searching and then discussion at a Church meeting it was decided in January 1972 to withdraw from the Baptist Union.

3.2 Prayer, Praise and Worship

Prayer and praise in many forms has been key to Church life. It is recorded that when Rev EW Tarbox laid the memorial stone in the first Church building in Goldsworth Road the celebration included an afternoon prayer and praise meeting. In 1952 members were circulated with a questionnaire concerning the prayer life of the Church. In 1960, when Philip Jones was the leader it is recorded that Friday night prayer meetings were held from 20.00 to midnight! For those who lived through the events during Harold's ministry none are likely to forget the prayer and Bible study meetings which were held in the Church "school room" in Percy Street. Around 100 people, from teenagers to those more mature in years, packed the room.

And when the Holy Spirit came the atmosphere was electric. The end of the meeting could not be limited to 21.30 or 22.00, and on some evenings it just went on and on. These hours were subsequently extended to some all-night prayer sessions when the Holy Spirit broke into Church life – but more about this in the next chapter.

Worship, music and song have always played a major role in Church services. During the period covered by this book the Church has used the *Baptist Hymn Book*, *Redemption Hymnal*, our own, home-produced *For His Praise* song book, more recently less formal acetates and finally SongPro. Participation from individuals has varied from worship led by one person located at the front to the much more open style adopted today. For those readers who were around during and after the outpouring of the Holy Spirit the following first few words of songs will bring back many memories:

Abba Father let me be.... All over the world the Spirit is moving.... And can it be....Bind us together, Lord.... Bless the Lord O my soul.... He brought me to his banqueting table.... How great Thou art.... I stand amazed.... I will enter His gates with thanksgiving in my heart.

Alice Potter records that "During the early days of the outpouring of the Holy Spirit in the 1970s; her husband Barry, who had been the Organist for many years, found himself more and more leaving the organ loft during evening services to play the grand piano alongside the pulpit because many of the songs were started by people in the congregation and were not suitable for a pipe organ accompaniment. Then Barry himself became filled with the Holy Spirit. For the first time ever, he was able to pick up the songs that were being sung from the congregation and lead us into the next verse in the correct key. Never before had he been able to play by ear and without music".

3.3 Evangelism

Evangelism has always played a key role in the life of the Church. From the earliest days of Rev Tarbox, outreach was on the agenda. Initially this took the form of establishing a Church presence in 1881 in Knap Hill (more recently spelt Knaphill) and then at the small community at Anthony's (near the Six Cross Roads in Woodham on the way to the M25) where it was found that "the folk were practically heathen, with the little folk running wild, the people ignorant of the gospel and their elders mostly engaged in gardening and debauchery". Evangelism for those away from the Woking area really started in 1887 when Rev Edward Tarbox announced to the members that in his opinion "the time had arrived when we as a Church should take an interest in mission work in the 'foreign' field". A special collection was held for the general fund of the Baptist Missionary Society for the support of widows and orphans of missionaries.

Over the years local evangelism has taken on many different formats from the group of young men who literally got on their bicycles and held open air meetings in Pirbright, to taking a leading role in October 1966 in the "Top Gear" young people's evangelistic campaign which included free coffee, taped and live Christian pop music and gospel presentations. The venue for the event was the top floor of HW Gloster's Warehouse in Church Street. Outside Woking the Church has sent and supported numerous members, from Cynthia Goodall and Peter and

Sunny Murray in the 1960s, to more recently Chris and Friederike Cliff, Paul and Debbie Abraham, David and Debbie Kimani, Luke Simone, and many others.

One of the most successful periods of international evangelism commenced in the early 1960s. The seeds of this work commenced in February 1960, when members at a Church meeting authorised the purchase of amplifying, tape recording and radio equipment. On 22 October 1962 the Wondrous Story Radio Mission was set up as a specific department of the Church.

News of this new method of outreach soon reached the Woking News and Mail and they included the following article in the local paper on 9 November 1962. The piece was entitled, "Modern Method of Spreading the Gospel" and read as follows:

"Emphasis at Woking Baptist Church in recent months has been upon the harnessing of modern electronics to the spreading of the gospel.

When the minister (Philip Jones) arrived in Woking three years ago he formed a committee of enthusiastic menfolk to pursue the possibility of extension ministries through radio, recordings and G.P.O. relay circuits. The committee is now fully engaged in all three of these activities.

Every Friday evening a team of vocalists meets at the church in a specially constructed control room in the gallery while Philip Jones sits by another microphone with his script. On a red cue light from the recordist the "operation" begins, and another 15-minute programme in the church's series, goes into production.

At about six-weekly intervals the master tapes are copied and sent out to two missionary radio stations - ELWA in Liberia, West Africa (operated by Sudan Interior Mission) and the network of the Far East Broadcasting Company in the Philippines (a non-profit Christian organisation). From these stations the programmes are transmitted at weekly intervals. Due to the need for allowing time for transit, etc., programmes are recorded sometimes as much as six months before the date of transmission.

In each programme an accommodation address in London is given to which listeners are invited to write. While there never has been a flood of letters, a steady five or six a week, telling of spiritual problems and requesting Gospel literature, arrive in Woking, where they are dealt with promptly by folk appointed by the deacons who have experience in counselling work.

The church is also using the G.P.O. closed circuit relay system whereby the two Sunday services and the Thursday evening Bible School are made available to the "shut-ins" and others unable to come to the church, at several listening points in the town.

Members of the committee man the controls in the booth and attend to the maintenance of the equipment."

In September 1981 it was announced at a Church meeting that with the Church's changing needs Wondrous Story Radio outreach would cease at the end of the year. Since its early days the work had expanded considerably and had resulted in a substantial response from listeners around the world.

In more recent years a number of courses have been used at The Coign Church to help people explore the basics of Christianity. There was the "Just looking" course in the early 1980s and this was followed by the highly successful *Alpha* course, written by Holy Trinity Brompton Church in

London. An extract from the *Alpha* web site describes the course as:

> *"A series of interactive sessions where anyone can explore life and the Christian faith in a friendly, open and informal environment"*

Alpha has been run at The Coign two or three times a year for around twenty years. Assuming an average attendance of twenty visitors per course, over eight hundred have taken part. The courses have been led by Nick Sharp, Phil Moore, Graham Allen, James Mellor and Dub Everitt. In recent years Tony Lynch became involved in running the *Beta* course as a follow-up to Alpha, and now Darren and Lois Forsdyke have introduced *Freedom in Christ* for those who want to deepen their Christian faith.

There are many in the Church today who have become Christians through Alpha and now live changed lives. Ask around the Church; it won't take long before you can find those with exciting stories.

CHAPTER 4

HOLY SPIRIT OUTPOURING

One of the most significant events in the history of the Church in Woking occurred during the late 1960s and its impact remains with us until the time of writing this book and hopefully will continue to do so. The third person of the Trinity (The Holy Spirit) broke through into the life of the Church initially through Harold, then through the Young People's Group and finally into the main body of the Church. This breakthrough changed our worship from "black and white" into "glorious technicolour". We experienced many of the gifts of the Holy Spirit as seen in the New Testament, prayer meetings became exciting (and lengthy) and many people became Christians. Bryan Cross

Welcome, Coign and Woking Baptist Church Story gives an account of the start of the work in the Young People's Group and David Dennington takes over the story and describes his own encounter with The Holy Spirit.

4.1 Initial breakthrough

Bryan records events as follows: "Shortly before I became a Church member on 1st September 1968 Harold had been away to a University Students' gathering and God had met many of the students and filled them with the Holy Spirit, something that was new to many of us. At the following Tuesday night prayer meeting the Pastor shared what had happened. Afterwards there was a feeling among a few of the young men that they would like to hear more. Peter Smith arranged with the Pastor for the young men to meet with him three days later on the Friday evening in the Upper Room, as it was called at that time. The Pastor invited two Church members (David Kirkland and David Parsons) to come with him as they had both had similar experiences of the Holy Spirit. From memory because the meeting was arranged at very short notice, only about five or six young men were able to attend. The Pastor shared with us about the Holy Spirit and referred to various passages in the scriptures about His working and the manifestations of the Spirit. He then got us, individually, to read through Psalm 51 and to ask God to cleanse us from our sin and ensure that we were right before Him. We were then encouraged to ask God to fill us. Each had to seek God individually, but the Pastor was there to help. During that evening and over the next few days God met us in a very special way. The following evening was the Young People's Coffee Bar and I believe that was the first night that someone became a Christian. Following these events, the Holy Spirit transformed the work amongst other Christian young people who were part of the Coffee Bar and many became Christians in a relatively short space of time, and then it began to spill over into other areas of the Church. Whilst this new and exciting work was gladly accepted by many of the members, others were much more cautious, and some felt compelled to leave the Church and worship elsewhere".

4.2 A Charismatic Church

David Dennington describes what happened to him and others in the period following the initial breakthrough of

The Holy Spirit into the life of the Church. "By 1971 a number of folk in the Woking Baptist Church had been baptised in the Spirit, mostly young people. They would meet on a Friday night for a prayer meeting and became known by other church members as the 'Holier than thou group' or just 'The God Squad'. Harold was taking a slowly slowly approach but was troubled by a group of members who, whilst not actively trying to remove him as Pastor, were certainly not cooperating.

"Harold made what turned out to be a significant move by arranging a Saturday Special teaching event at The Capel Bible College on Saturday 2 October 1971 with Charlie Pocock and George Tarleton as guest speakers. 50 church members attended the day; the bait was that the young people volunteered to occupy our children for the day. The teaching was promised to be strictly Bible based. We had three children and took the bait! The first session centred on The Holy Spirit and Scripture (this was Scriptural, interesting and we could not argue with that). After coffee we had a session on the gifts of the Spirit (this was based on Scripture so we could not argue with that either). After a very good lunch we had a session on the Baptism in the

Spirit, commencing in the Gospel of Luke, moving on to the book of Acts and then into 1 Corinthians Chapter 12. At the end of this session a surprise announcement was made to the effect that after the afternoon cup of tea we were now free to go home unless we wanted to be prayed for to receive the Baptism in the Holy Spirit. We were instructed that we should walk in the garden and only talk to our spouses during the break.

"Shirley (my wife) and I decided that we did not need to receive this offer but did not wish to leave our friends, who much to our disappointment went into the conference room two by two until we were the last to be in the garden. Reluctantly we went in, only to find that the last two empty chairs were in the front row. As soon as we sat down Charlie Pocock said, 'Would the front row please kneel down'. Wow! George and Charlie started at the end of the row. When Charlie prayed for the person next to me, he went off like a rocket speaking in tongues, frightening the living daylights out of me. George came to me. I knew nothing would happen and waited for him to finish. He suggested I should relax. No way! At last he said, "You can go now". Charlie prayed for Shirley and we were greatly relieved to get out and go home.

"After we had been in the car for a few minutes on the road to Abinger Hammer (near Dorking) we realised we were singing loudly, Shirley was singing old Welsh hymns and I was driving in a really crazy dangerous manner. The car felt as if it was floating and I was driving on both sides of the road. It took a while for us to realise we were absolutely drunk. We didn't speak in tongues but we just couldn't stop singing. Curiously when we stopped singing out loud we could still hear the singing going on inside us. We got home, didn't sleep much that night and were then in that "high" state for about a week. We did not speak in tongues until about 18 months later. Sometimes it is said that you cannot be baptised in the Spirit if you don't really want to be. We know that is not true. We just got taken by the scruff of the neck. Yes, we knelt down, yes, we let them pray for us but, no we did not want to be baptised. But to this day we praise God that He got us. It changed our whole life, it changed our marriage. It changed our family; it changed our whole way of living.

"Following the Capel Training day when so many individuals were baptised in the Spirit I felt that the Church itself got baptised in the Spirit. Over the coming months a number of changes began to happen. Worship changed from just hymn singing, I remember the first time we heard singing in the Spirit, Tuesday night Bible studies began to go through prophetic subjects and unfortunately, we began to see a few folk leave the Church (in total there were only about 12). The governance of the church was changed, Deacons all stepped down, and the Elders took their primary biblical role."

We had become a Charismatic Baptist Church!

4.3 Monochrome to Colour

For many of those privileged to be in the Church during the period described above, one of the outstanding manifestations of the Holy Spirit was the change in our desire and ability to worship. Worship has always been a fundamental aspect of Church life but somehow it took on new dimensions. Simply stated, it changed from monochrome to colour. Meetings were exciting and often unpredictable either in content or duration. Pippa Osborn

Welcome, Coign and Woking Baptist Church Story gives her testimony to this life- changing experience of the outpouring of the Holy Spirit:

"My family and I moved to Woking in early 1969 after spending my first 16 years in Central and East Africa. I joined the young people's group. I had a real faith, but it was fairly formal and conservatively evangelical. Some of the girls at school invited me to the Christian coffee bar run by the young people of the Church - it was amazing! In that dimly lit somewhat murky atmosphere on Saturday evenings, I met Christians my own age who had had an excitingly real experience of God through the Holy Spirit and an intoxicating love for Jesus. My rather serious black and white faith was transformed into glorious technicolour and my life totally changed. Looking back, I praise God for the friends I made and the patience and support of the leaders".

God made his presence felt in many ways including through the prophetic word. Whilst many of these experiences are only available in individual memories, some have survived the years, having been recorded in written form in the weekly church bulletin variously named

"Announcer", "Newsletter" or "The Coign Messenger". In these documents the Editors, which included David Kirkland, Vera O'Brian, Pat Checksfield, Derrick Ball, Len Chart and Chas Davis, sought to capture God's word for his Church. Here are a few extracts from some of these documents:

"My children, I am teaching you that healing, to Me, is of the whole man and so much of the needs of men and women today even their physical sicknesses are the outcome of tortured minds, unhappy hearts, of bitter spirits and of broken relationships. As you have already prayed my children I will make this people a people of healing and into this community of people I desire to bring those who are sick not only in body but in mind and spirit and in heart. I will bring broken marriages and heal them. I will bring unhappy relationships between parents and children and make them afresh. I will heal families. I will heal homes. I will heal lives and I will heal bodies as I see fit. My children, this is what I would do amongst you and that is why I am causing you to wait upon Me and not to run ahead of me and not to think you know the answers for I am wanting you to learn a deep lesson – for if I am to be the Healer among you, you must be a healed people." (5 June 1977.)

"It is my purpose to change you, to change you into the image of my dear Son to make you increasingly like unto Him, not on your efforts but on My Grace... I will call you to a holy dissatisfaction ... But oh, my people there is much more that I desire and that I purpose to do in your hearts and lives. My purpose and will is that you should be changed and if you resist the change in your own life, then My Spirit is grieved and quenched and yet I will have my way with you... I desire to see you as I have created you..." (7 September 1975.)

"My children, hell's foundations quiver at the shout of praise, but I want you now to be aware because I have a great purpose for you as my people. Great purposes in this area... Holland ... Lands of which, as yet, you have not thought ... For I have great things to do and my enemy and your enemy is aware of this and he is on the attack, and he is going to attack you as you have never been attacked before. On every level you are going to know attacks ... I allow this. Not that you should go under, but that you should come up; not that you should yield to the enemy's attacks, but as you have just been doing so you should learn to meet every attack with a shout of praise … For in that praise not only will hell's foundations quiver, but the gates of hell shall fall flat before My Kingdom people." (12 February 1978)

"Children, you have just sung the song of triumph and it is a battle hymn though you do not realise it. I am calling My Church to be a people terrible as an army with banners. I am calling My people to assemble themselves together, that in unity they might come against my enemy and theirs. I do call you in the coming days to warfare that shall be bloody and warfare that shall be costly. Each one of you who calls yourself by my name has enlisted under my banner. It is a banner of love, but it is also the banner of my righteousness and my holy purposes…. I will call you each one to be willing to lay down your lives, your interests, your hobbies and your time. Lay down whatever I require that you might be good soldiers of Jesus Christ. So arise indeed and go forth to war, even now claim the victory for I guarantee it." (22 June 1982)

"I am bringing to an end one chapter and starting another. Let go. Turn the page and let God start writing the new chapter. The chapter will involve pain as the Spirit broods over you and deals with you. So decide again who you will serve. Before you, are set days of great joy as well as pain; the pain because a visitation of my holiness will come, which some areas of your life cannot stand. My Church will be clean, holy and pure. Will you allow me to come and visit, even though the cost will be great?" (May 1987.)

4.4 Governance

Up until the appointment of Michael Maughan in November 1973 as full time Elder assisting Harold, the oversight of the Church was primarily the responsibility of the lead Pastor, with more practical matters referred to the Church at regular Church meetings. With the outpouring of the Holy Spirit it was decided to run the Church along the lines given in the New Testament where a group of Elders were responsible for the spiritual growth and development of the Church and Deacons, responsible for the practical aspects of the work. This, combined with an increasing commitment both at home and overseas and increased membership, meant that it was not possible, or sensible, for all matters to rest on the shoulders of one person.

Within a few years of the outpouring of The Holy Spirit there was a substantial increase in the number of full-time staff, each with an area of responsibility. This is how it worked out in practice:

Harold Owen - Preaching in Woking, UK ministry (including Crawley, Durham and Sheffield), overseas ministry (including Holland, Switzerland and Austria) and a 20% "time tithe" (a percentage of his own time)

Howard Dodge - Oversee Church administration, Secretary to the Elders, production of Bible reading notes for Church attendees, Preaching and a 10% "time tithe" for other UK churches problem solving and Uganda

David Dennington - Counselling, prayer ministry, visiting and a 10% "time tithe" for gypsies, Holland and Austria

David Brown - Bible teaching and Uganda and a 10% "time tithe" for New Frontiers

Sean Larkin - Preaching and ministry

Ray Booth - Preaching and supporting Harold.

4.5 New Expressions of Worship

Traditionally we had about five hymns pre-selected and put up on the two boards either side of the pulpit. Each hymn would have four or five verses. The hymn was sung once. Various things were fitted between the hymns: the offering, the notices, Bible readings, activity reports, Church news items etc. Sometimes this procedure was called "The hymn sandwich". It was praise but not worship as we might understand it today. There was a period of experimentation with an appointed worship leader and with the introduction of a variety of musical instruments. As the style of musical accompaniment and content changed, it gave opportunity for younger members to join music groups. In order to have some control over the musical expertise of the musicians they had to get to Grade 8 and also had to be able to play by ear. By the time we moved to The Coign we had a distinctive "Coign" style. The worship leader or lead musician would start the worship with one song. This would then lead into open worship when others in the congregation would start a new song, pray, sometimes prophesy, sometime speak out in tongues or read scripture. It was a fascinating thing to experience the development of all manner of themes and wonderful experiences of the presence of God. Sometimes the younger girls and teenagers, individually or together would worship in dance; this brought a beautiful expression of worship and devotion. After we moved into the Coign building the (empty) baptistry was left open to be a feature and demonstrate that baptism was available. However after a child fell in, it was decided to keep the covers on.

4.6 Spontaneous Baptisms

Spontaneous baptisms in water took place in the early 1970's, similar in ways to the story recorded about Philip and the Ethiopian Eunuch in the New Testament. Following a baptismal service at The Coign an invitation was given for people who were already trusting in Jesus Christ for salvation to be baptised in obedience to his command. Not only was there a response but some wanted to be baptised straight away. Two such examples were Liesbeth and George van Muiswinkel, a Dutch couple who were shortly returning to Holland. They had been baptised in the Holy Spirit during their time at Percy Street. Their testimonies were known to the Eldership and they agreed to baptise them then and there. There was some hasty scuttling around for some baptismal clothes!

Howard Dodge recorded that our monthly third Sunday evening baptisms did not miss a month for the first six years in the Coign building.

4.7 All things in common

In the New Testament the initial outpouring of the Holy Spirit impacted directly on the lives of the believers. Not only was there an increase in the numbers of people who believed or were healed but people's attitude to possessions also changed. Brian Bonnington describes what happened to him, his family and others in the Church. They believed that God was asking a group of them to live together in a communal house in Woking. Here they could experience the benefits of communal living and make room for those who needed help. Brian and Joan take up their story:

"We purchased 'Ichthys', a seven bedroomed house, near the centre of Woking, in December 1974 with John and Hazel Pearce and Bryan Cross. Initially the purchase arrangements progressed smoothly but, on the day of the move, problems developed, and a miracle was needed if the move was to go ahead. We had all intended to sell our houses and pool the money. By the time of completion of contracts only our house in Woodham had been sold so, on the day of completion, Brian and Hazel went along to our solicitor John Ogden to tell him that we could not complete as two of the houses had not even exchanged, and without exchange we couldn't get a bridging loan to get us in. They arrived at his office and John had to phone our vendor's solicitor to tell him that completion could not take place due to lack of funds. He replied that his client understood the situation and because he trusted us he, the vendor, was happy to lend us the £14,000 we needed to get into the house and we could pay him back as soon as the other houses sold. The key, he said, was under a tub by the front door!!! John, I think was astounded and, we, of course, could see God's hand in it all and gratefully accepted the loan. By February 1975 all the houses had sold, and we were able to pay back the loan and the interest on it, which was at a much lower rate than would have been required by the bank.

"We lived together pooling all our resources including cars, possessions etc. and lived communally as a household, hoping that in so doing we would be able to open our home and help those in need, as well as learning to live together as an extended family. Our children Mark and Stuart were 11 and 8 when we moved in and John and Hazel had their first baby Joanna in September 1976. Bryan moved out to marry Helen and Brenda Nearn and her daughter moved in. In 1977 Peter and Angela Smith came to us for about 6 months whilst she was having her second baby as she had had difficulties with her first.

"The following year John and Hazel felt it was time for them to set up home as a family on their own and Rick and Lynne Hewitt moved in whilst they were between houses. They stayed for about 18 months and Brian and I felt that we should sell the house and move into our own home once again. It had been a very special time. Sometimes difficult but, on reflection, we learnt so much about each other and particularly about ourselves. We saw God at work in many miraculous ways and we still feel it was a very special time in our lives"

Not all members adopted the same solution about what the Lord was calling them to do. Some decided to only keep what was needed and gave the rest away.

4.8 Testimonies

A number of miraculous manifestations of the Holy Spirit were experienced in Harold's time in Woking. Unfortunately, it is not possible to record all of them in this book, but I have included the following - firstly, Edie Nunn's testimony, recorded in October 1997, and secondly, the story of Mark and Alison Young. This is followed by several very different testimonies, all of which demonstrate God's most miraculous power.

4.8.1 Edith Nunn

"I grew up in Portsmouth and moved to Woking in 1965 due to my mother being ill and so she could have someone with her in the home while I was at work. For a number of years I'd had a limp and, in 1970, my left leg was dragging and my left arm became affected and very weak. I was sent for a radioactive brain scan in London as they were querying a brain tumour. In 1971 I went for a lumbar puncture, EEG and visual tests and was given the diagnosis of Multiple Sclerosis. First, I was on one stick, two sticks then elbow crutches. Then I had a major relapse and had to go into a wheelchair full-time. I was no longer able to use the crutches. I was unable to bath myself, at times it was difficult to feed myself and I was going into hospital for respite care every 6 weeks, staying at least 2 weeks. My sight was poor and general deterioration in my condition made it difficult to stay at home, even with the help of a district nurse. In 1988 it became clear that I needed to look for residential accommodation. Unfortunately, there was nothing in Woking, so I had to go to Leatherhead where they had a home for disabled people. It was by then harder to cope with routine things. I was unable to read or watch television and used an electric typewriter with arm supports. I was very unhappy in the home. I felt rejected, isolated and generally very sad. My condition continued to deteriorate, despite the fact that I was prayed for many times, but not healed. I was given peace and the ability to feed myself came back, but I was not healed of the MS.

"In June 1991 I was taken to a healing service and I went hoping my sight would be healed. The man who was speaking, Martin Scott, said that he believed there were three people there with hiatus hernias and if they put their hands up the people around them would pray and they would be healed. Now, I'd had one for 17 years, but I wasn't very brave and I didn't put my hand up very high, and then he became more specific and he said there was somebody in the block where I was sitting. I was braver then. I put my hand up higher, and God healed me, which was good although I had learnt to live with it. I was able to lie down at night and also to eat food I'd had problems with before. Then in August 1991 I had a chest and throat infection and my voice went. Unfortunately, despite speech therapy it did not return, and I needed to wear an amplifier. This caused a lot of mockery in the home, especially in the dining room with 24 other people, there were difficulties, and I had to get the funds to buy my own. I just had it for three days when I was told there was another healing service, on February 23 1992. By then I had had enough of going to healing services, I was very low, I'd gone through a very bad patch and so I said to the Lord, "If you want me there, you provide the transport. I'm not asking for anyone to take me". The offer came just 6 hours before the service.

This meant that I had to go to bed for the whole afternoon in order to be able to go out in the evening. It was again Martin Scott speaking, and he spoke on the leper being healed, and he said the Lord had told him there will be someone there with MS and if they came forward he would pray because the Lord wanted to heal them. Although he had no idea who I was, Martin turned and smiled at me, and there were at least a dozen people there in wheel chairs. My friends took me forward and I was prayed for. At first nothing happened except I shook from head to foot, then Martin went away, came back and prayed again and this time I took about 3 steps with his help, then the Holy Spirit came upon me very powerfully, and I went down on the floor. When I came to I felt wonderful but I wasn't able to get up so they had to pick me up and put me in my wheelchair again. But Martin did say he believed I would be walking by the end of the week. By the time I returned to my friend's car my voice had returned. I had not spoken properly for 6 months. That to me was a clear sign the Lord was fulfilling His promise to heal me.

"Next day I started standing and walking a little. As you can imagine at first it was quite painful because my legs had not taken weight for 15 years and also, because my knees were straight, my balance was off. It all sorted itself out and I had no physiotherapy to help me whatsoever, I just relied on the Lord and He did as He promised. On the Saturday, just one day short of the week I walked along the corridor, went down in the lift and walked into the dining room where I was living. 9 weeks later I went for tests to see if I could have my driving licence returned. I saw a psychologist, an eye specialist, physiotherapist, and went in a simulator for tests, then saw a doctor. The doctor said he could not understand it because with the tests he did, there was no sign whatsoever of the MS. On my notes it said I had MS. I tried to explain to him about my healing but there were problems. I was still getting used to the idea too. Afterwards he told me that he was an atheist.

"When I returned to the home I was given 6 months' notice to get out. I had no home and no furniture. I applied to move back into Woking but that was refused so I had to move into a flat in Leatherhead. This was just 10 minutes' walk from the home and I was able to go back once a week and do voluntary book keeping there, which was the job I'd done before. When I received my allowance books in the flat I found that although I was living alone and doing everything for myself they were still paying me full time attendance allowance and mobility allowance. There was no way I could keep the money because it would be denying what God had done. So I contacted the authorities about returning it. The local office said they could not deal with it because, after all, especially with the attendance allowance, when you qualify for the full time one you are not supposed to recover, but eventually they agreed that I didn't qualify and took it all back. If I had kept the mobility allowance I could have run a car, but it's given God the glory for what He's done, that's the chief thing. It was not easy returning to a normal life with just a week to do it in. After all, as you become disabled you adjust mentally to each stage when things are difficult, but when you are suddenly restored to full health in one week it's very difficult to adjust to it all. And during the time I was ill there had been many hurts. I had to learn to bath myself, I hadn't done that for 19 years; to cross a road, to get on a bus and to do all the things we don't think about when we're fit and well.

"In July 1993 I went on a Hildenborough Trust holiday to Torquay and the theme for the week was 'Living through Change', which I had certainly done, and during that week the Lord took down the wall I had built around my emotions to save some of the hurt. At first I felt very vulnerable and it was painful, but the Lord took over and He is in control. It means that now I can use my healing to help other people.

"In March 1994 I moved back to Woking. I now have an upstairs flat with no lift and I'm back near my friends, family and church, which is wonderful.

"When invited to do so, I go to other places, giving my testimony, telling what God has done in my life in the hope of encouraging and helping others.

"In October 1995 a book entitled "Miracles" by Geoff and Hope Price was published and the story of my healing was included. My G.P. from 1974, who is not a Christian, made a contribution and allowed his name to be included. He is quoted in the book as stating 'the MS was proven by several neurologists and her prognosis was poor'. He concluded by stating my "recovery is full and unexplained". Several copies of the book have been made available in the Surrey libraries.

"I do not know why God healed me after 21 years, why I had to wait so long, or why He does not heal other people, but I just want to use my healing now to serve Him and to help others and give Him the glory for what He has done. I know He has a plan for each of us and we can only trust Him for each day and His timing to fulfil His purposes for us all".

4.8.2 The Young family

Chris Young recalls one of three miracles which took place in her family:

"In August 1979 we experienced a horrific car accident at the end of the school holiday. From the moment the car stopped I knew God's peace, even though both children were seriously injured and my mother too. Mark had a severe head injury and was transferred to The Atkinson Morley Brain Injury hospital in Wimbledon. Alison was admitted to intensive care with a badly smashed face, a broken arm, cuts on her hand and lip, needing stitches and internal injuries. We were told that there was no way they could stabilize the loose bones in her face, eye sockets and jaw, so as she healed and grew they would need to do corrective surgery on the deformities as they developed. One evening as we left Intensive Care we had to sign the operation consent form for her to have her spleen removed. She was deteriorating to the point when they would have to operate. When we arrived home our group leaders were waiting for us and we started to pray for Alison. In the morning when we went back to the hospital we learnt that she had stopped deteriorating and the operation had not occurred. When I checked the notes, I found the time she had stopped deteriorating was exactly the time we had prayed the night before. Mark meanwhile was in a coma paralysed down his right side and we were told that he may not survive and even if he did he would be severely brain damaged. The Church was praying for us and on the Sunday had joined hands across the congregation to pray. They continued to pray during the week and at one of these meetings James Mellor prayed, “In the name of Jesus, Mark I tell you to wake up.” From that evening Mark started to slowly regain consciousness. Alison has never had to have corrective surgery on her face and she still has her spleen!! Mark has had no lasting damage except that he lost the hearing and balance in his left ear. We were told that another blow to his head would be fatal and that he should not do contact sports, climb trees, ride a bike etc. We believed God had healed him and insisted he was allowed to be a 'normal' boy especially at school. Shortly after returning to school he was given a judo flip in the playground resulting in his head hitting the playground quite hard and he had 5 stitches in his head. The school were in panic, blaming me for my irresponsibility in insisting that he be allowed in the playground and when we arrived at the hospital they couldn't understand why he was OK either!! - Our God showed his proof of healing!!! We were able to go briefly to The Coign evening service with both children to thank God for his healing and goodness to us after the accident!! Praise the Lord!!"

4.8.3 An Irish lady

David Dennington recalls an unusual prayer session that he and Ray Booth were involved in. "We met up with a Pastor from another Church and a lady member from his congregation. She was Irish, a very angry and verbal lady. Sufficient here to say she had had a very difficult childhood in Ireland. When she told her story, she held her handbag very tightly on her lap. Our usual procedure was firstly to listen to both her and her Pastor, we would ask a few questions and then if we were ready and in full agreement we would pray, perhaps anoint with oil. On this occasion I felt that it was important for her to forgive her father. Eventually she was reluctantly ready. We asked her to kneel down by her chair, and out loud she asked God to forgive her father. Part way through she stopped and shouted "NO I WANT MY GUN". You need to know that this happened at the time of the IRA troubles. We all looked around for her handbag..... it could not be seen. Where was the gun? This is a very angry lady – find the gun. It was safely in the handbag between her knees. I, in my strongest deliverance voice, said "Get on with your prayer, you cannot have your gun". Surprisingly she continued with her prayer. Eventually we were able to say that we had been witness of her confession and prayers and we can assure her of forgiveness. She got up from the floor, her face full of smiles and joy, thanked us all and said "I'm sorry about my outburst. I thought I was going to have an asthma attack and would need my Ventolin". She and her pastor never needed to come for more prayer.

4.8.4 The Occult

Harold developed a close pastoral relationship with the white witch leader and her husband from a local coven. They both committed their lives to Christ. David Dennington was asked to take on the teaching; they would need to change their lives around. They had a huge collection of occult books and occult artefacts which they eventually decided to burn. David writes, "John Forrest and I were called upon to perform this service. The collection filled John's estate car. He obtained a mobile furnace and we found an old army camp where there were concrete slabs where we could not be observed or disturbed. As we unloaded, we separated the hard items of glass, crystal pendants, brass divination discs, ornaments and effigies putting them on the concrete block away from the furnace. We were about a hundred yards from the nearest building. No one came to see us. When we had the furnace well alight and burning we went to get the hard items from about 15 feet away. Every hard item had disappeared; completely gone, vanished into thin air. We knew then that we were dealing with something very powerful."

David notes that he was surprised how many of our members had occult connections, had had sessions with fortune telling and tarot. Occasionally they were asked if they had any lucky charms, copper bracelets, anchor crosses etc. If the items were given to him, he would drop them in the river on his way home.

CHAPTER 5

AN EXPANDING MISSION FIELD

Whilst evangelism has always been a key ministry within the Church, when the Holy Spirit started to impact the lives of Church members a renewed enthusiasm and sense of importance of this spread across the Church. Recorded below are four very different examples of how the good news of Jesus was taken to the people of Woking and then further afield. Dr. James Mellor and David Dennington tell us about a one-off meeting during the course of a doctor's work that led to many gypsies becoming Christians. Tony Lyttle records a Church evangelistic campaign, David Dennington describes what happened when a cup of coffee was offered to a stranger and David Field, a telephone help line for those in need.

5.1 A Doctor Called

"In 1981 some Romany families parked their caravans on common ground in Horsell. The matriarch of the families, Esther, consulted me (James) regarding some serious health issues and was referred to a hospital consultant. They called me to visit her after seeing the consultant who had told her she was dying, and no further treatment was possible. She was obviously distressed and, during my conversation with her, expressed her fear of dying. I explained to her and her family that she could be forgiven for all she had done wrong and receive God's free gift of eternal life, so that she could go to be with Jesus after she died. She gladly accepted this message and asked me to pray with her to become a Christian. The rest of the family were sent out of the caravan but flocked round the van looking in at the windows, while Esther made her peace with God. The joy of the Lord must have been evident on Esther's face because her daughter accused me of slipping her a Mickey Finn!".

A few weeks later Henry, Esther's husband, committed his life to Christ and both were filled with the Holy Spirit.

This was the beginning of many Romany people coming to the Lord and regularly attending The Coign. They were also very zealous evangelists visiting Romany sites all around the area and bringing many of their own people to God. (They preferred the word "vandalising" to "evangelising"!)

James records some of the highlights of this time when the Holy Spirit moved in the Romany group: "Esther's baptism, when she managed to get out of her wheelchair into the pool and out again; her husband Henry being baptised just a few days before Esther's death; Esther's funeral at The Coign with about 200 Romany people attending; the sight of seven vehicles laden with flowers accompanying her funeral cortege; one of her daughters being restrained from jumping into her mother's grave; visiting the wake at the Hatch' N' Tan with the family".

David records his memories of the work amongst the Romanies: "At the same time as the events described above, French Gypsies came to the Derby and led Billy

Bower, from Chobham, to the Lord. She started to come to The Coign Church. She was well known in the Gypsy community as a horse breaker. Henry and I (David) would travel around the gypsy community within Surrey and later some of Kent.

“Esther’s funeral opened the way into the wider family. News of The Coign Church spread throughout the gypsy world and on a Sunday night they would drive from as far away as Birmingham and Gravesend, Slough, and a group from Darlington. One separate group worked Canada in the summer and returned to Shepherds Bush in the winter and regarded us as their UK Church.

“We were asked to attend the Leatherhead site and form a house group. The Elders asked Jim and Christine Cousins to take on the group and later Janet and Mike Phipps also came on board. Christine started to teach the women to read. We would baptise them in the river Mole behind the site and the gypsies even got the local council to change the name of their road to Salvation Way.

“Shirley, my wife, and I had a caravan which we ‘pulled’ with the gypsies to their conventions and gatherings. I acted as Elder/Pastor which at that time they needed before they had started training up their own folk. Other Coign folk helped out and notably John Ogden was an unlikely but much-loved encourager in the community. He would come to gypsy meetings in his suit and tie and generally his only verbal contribution would be that they would ask him to pray, which he did with great aplomb accompanied by many loud 'amens'.

"The gypsies were people of great faith and there are many stories of healings and amazing conversions, from bare knuckle fighters and thieves and robbers (and worse!)"

5.2 A Cup of Coffee

Another example of evangelism, which had wide geographical implications, started one day with a simple cup of coffee. David Dennington takes up the story: "Pat and Len Chart lived in a small house in Kingfield with their four children. Pat liked to talk to folk in the street and one day met a Dutch lady; they chatted, and Pat invited Pia to come home for a cup of coffee. During the conversation Pat invited Pia to come to her Wednesday morning Bible study.

Pia agreed that she would like to come, but could she bring her friend Lizbeth with her?

"Pia and Lizbeth started to come to Woking Baptist Church with their husbands Fred and George. They joined the new home groups and were subsequently baptised. The husbands both worked for Shell Oil at Waterloo and eventually after a couple of years completed their tours. Fred and Pia returned to Reeuwijk in Holland, and George and Lizbeth initially returned to Holland and later to Curacao before returning to Berkel in Holland.

"Pia and Fred started a youth group in Reeuwijk, George and Lizbeth started a home group in their home town of Berkel. This home group eventually became the Vinestok Germeente Church, planted by Coign Elders and now part of Newfrontiers.

"Twenty-five years later some of the Reeuwijk youth group planted the Reeuwijk Community Church, part of Newfrontiers. Some of those original young people now serve in Wellington, New Zealand; some are running a substantial orphan work for street children in Brazil and some work with orphan children in Holland.

"At the final two Stoneleigh Bible Weeks, twenty plus years later, the Dutch contingent numbered some 600-folk coming from six churches in Holland travelling by cars and ferries and some by bicycles. Where did they come from? Well, it all started with a cup of coffee."

5.3 Come, See a Man

In the early days of the Holy Spirit's revitalizing His people, Tuesday evening prayer meetings were exciting occasions. Tony Lyttle records what happened on one of these evenings: "One Tuesday in December 1973, Vic Robertson shared what he felt God was telling him, that we should produce a musical presentation of what God is doing amongst us and link it to a telling of the Gospel story. I told him after the meeting that I also had on my heart the desire to tell the gospel in modern song and had already written a couple of pieces. From that beginning, the concept was developed of presenting Jesus and all He did, in a series of songs, interspersed with testimonies from people in the Church showing how He is still doing, today, the miracles He did in New Testament times. A few nights later, while praying about the idea, the story of the

Samaritan woman at the well, as recorded in John Chapter 4 verses 1 to 42, came into my mind. Having met with Jesus, in her enthusiasm she wanted all her friends to come and get to know Him, too – which was our desire as well. We wanted to share our experience of Him and help others to meet with Him and come to know His touch on their own lives. The title for our production seemed to jump out at me. It was obvious, Come, See a Man!

"Hester Clarke (who did the artwork for the invitation to the event) had the idea of opening with a brief drama about the Samaritan woman, which she went on to produce. It ended with the woman, played by Lynne Hewitt, entreating her friends to 'Come, see a Man that told me everything I have ever done!' A choir, formed for the occasion, immediately took up the theme with the opening number, 'Come, see a Man… our Lord and Saviour, Jesus Christ'. The songs then continued the narrative, starting with Jesus' birth in Bethlehem and going right through to His death and resurrection and ending with the celebratory, 'The Holy Ghost has come... and we are not the same anymore!' before a final reprise of 'Come, See a Man' this time including the directly challenging line: 'Oh now, won't you come and see Jesus Christ?'

"Throughout the presentation the singing was shared between the choir and a guitar group that consisted of Sally Hayllar (now Woods), Dot Blee, John Carr, Malcolm Watling and myself. Soloists in the choir included Aileen Owers, Marion Sheffield and me. Dot Blee and myself wrote all the songs and I produced the script for the drama and the links between the episodes, whether song or testimony. We used scriptures and some narration to introduce the various accounts from Church members about God's healings, miraculous provision and rescue from life's storms that they had each experienced personally.

"Alice Potter arranged the pieces, trained and conducted the choir. There was a children's choir, too, led by Aileen. They sang a piece entitled, 'Jesus said, Let the little children come to me,' and this was followed by a child's testimony of how they came to Christ. We included a few simple worship choruses which everyone could join in. It was Derrick Ball, one of our Elders, who acted as narrator, holding it all together and presenting the challenge of the gospel at the end.

"*Come, See a Man* was first produced at Percy Street Baptist Church on Saturday 12th April, 1975. It was subsequently performed again to a larger audience at The Winston Churchill School on Saturday 24th January, 1976. On that occasion, Helen Dodge (now Cross) replaced Dot in the group and Mary Maughan sang one of the solos. For all who took part, *Come, See a Man* has had a lasting impact; it is still remembered fondly by many. We trust, too, that the impact it had on the lives of the people who attended the presentations has been as long-lasting and meaningful."

5.4 Help is Only a Phone Call Away

Another avenue for reaching out to those in need commenced towards the end of Harold's leadership at The Coign Church. David Field describes the origin and outworking of the Church help line: "In 1988 one of the leadership team, Sean Larkin, became aware of the growing number of people who sought prayer/counsel after the evening service. Sean then widened his concern to those outside the Church who were in need of help. His research led him to Plymouth where a group of churches had formed a daytime helpline. Having heard at first hand their experiences, he drew up a plan that the Elders agreed should be put to the Church members. At a meeting a large number volunteered to become 'Listeners' or 'Helpers' (a friendly euphemism for a counsellor).

"A training programme was devised at which Listeners were taught how to respond to callers. Their task was to be a 'listening ear'; not to get into a counselling role. Having understood the situation of the caller they would, if appropriate, offer to arrange a meeting with a Helper. At the beginning a room was made available at Brian Bonnington's home with the installation of two dedicated telephone lines (one in – one out) for the Listeners. In the early days the lines were manned in the mornings and 2 Listeners stayed in the control room for the night. Over time, changes were made in stages so that eventually the Helpline was open 24 hours. The use of the Control Room was phased out and replaced with a system to switch calls to the homes of Listeners or Helpers.

"If a caller welcomed the idea of a meeting, details about the call would be passed to the Helper on duty. Often callers just expressed their thanks for being able to talk to someone who appeared understanding.

"Instruction in the basics of counselling was given to the Helpers. It was preferable to meet with a caller at their home but, if not convenient or appropriate, the Coign building would be suggested, or a neutral venue. The reasons for calls covered a wide range of situations. Among those frequently expressed were problems within families, loneliness, anxieties about teenagers and financial difficulties: experience revealed that the problem first mentioned was not always the main one. Calls were often received late at night or even in the early hours of the morning.

"The majority of meetings with a Helper were one-off sessions that ended with a suggested action which the caller should find helpful. Occasionally follow up sessions were arranged for a period and then a review; in some cases, help was given over a longer period. There were also cases when friendships developed that proved fruitful and much valued.

"It was reported at the Annual Church Meeting that fourteen calls were received within the first two weeks of the help-line starting; seven had been trivial, four wanted to meet people at The Coign and one had attended a Sunday service. The following year one hundred people were involved as listeners or helpers and a hundred people had contacted the help-line. Eventually we began to notice the number of calls falling. The number of alternative help-lines available had increased. Also, the size of the Helpers team had shrunk, partly because The Coign had increased its range of ministries and, perhaps, expectations of the helpline had declined. In 1994 Brian Bonnington and I concluded the service had run its course. It had served its purpose well by helping a number of people and Listeners and Helpers had gained experience".

5.5 The Birth of House Groups

The formation of house groups and the end of the mid-week Bible study in the 1970s, just before we moved to the Methodist Church (a stopgap measure when Brewery Road

Methodist allowed us to hold our Sunday services there in the afternoons after we had to vacate Percy Street and before The Coign was built), was very significant in the life of the Church both at that time and for many years to come.

David Dennington records their birth:

"About a year before we left Percy Street, Harold set up a four-week series of men's meetings on a Sunday evening. Each evening had a theme e.g. the Christian man at work, in Church and in his marriage.

"Prior to the fourth week we were warned not to attend the final meeting unless we were prepared to commit our whole lives, spiritual, financial and sexual. In other words, everything to the Lord.

"When we were all in and counted there were exactly 100 men including Harold in the room. I think we signed in. Harold then outlined his plan for geographical groups. There would be ten men chosen by him and the Elders who would be the leaders of ten groups. The men who were present and had committed would be allocated to a leader. For the following three months the leaders would meet in the geographical areas and study again the four subjects.

After these weeks women married to men in the groups and those in committed relationships could join their menfolk and then lastly single ladies could join. Each group started with about 10 members.

"Group leaders were responsible for pastoral care, baptism preparation and membership interviews. We could break bread. All children of our members were considered to be members of the group and, if they wished, could attend group meetings. Our *Greenmeads* group grew to 48 members and on one occasion we had 44 members present (teenagers in the kitchen, twenties on the stairs and hall, children doing homework in the dining room and the remainder squeezed into the lounge.) They were very exciting times...we learnt to pray big prayers, prophesy and share our lives together. Eventually it was essential to appoint some more groups."

5.6 More Than a Meal

God moves in strange and mysterious ways. The seeds of another ministry were sown when Marks and Spencer moved in to Woking. Rather than throw away food which had reached its sell by date, the management wondered if

The Coign Church could help distribute it to those in need. This offer, combined with Nick and Penny Sharp's heart to help meet the needs of the marginalized in the local area, led to the birth of *Way In*. Soon a team of helpers, including the present-day leader Ann Elkins, was formed and readied for action.

In the early 1990s *Way In* opened its doors on a Good Friday lunch time to the unemployed and the homeless, to those with depression, addictions, mental health problems and the elderly and it continues to meet those in need to this day. Over a meal there is an opportunity to talk about their needs and, where appropriate, to hear the good news of Jesus. Those with specific needs are signposted to the relevant agencies.

A team of up to eight people help bring the food to the tables and engage with the men and women. Behind the scenes there are three who are responsible for cooking the food, two more for serving and two washers up.

Over the years weekly attendance has reached a maximum of eighty. Donors of suitable food have ranged from Marks and Spencer (who provided 4 turkeys and 12 lettuces for the first Good Friday lunch) through to Nando's, the current supplier of chicken but the Church, itself, buys much of it, too.

There are many stories which could be told but it is not wise to attribute these directly to individuals. However, to give a flavour, here are a few words and issues which have come up:

Samurai swords… Self-harm…. Ambulances… Armed police… Unemployment… No bank account… No permanent address… Alcohol… LifeShapers… Baptism… Family links… Death… Sleeping in car in Church carpark … Debt… Scared after word of knowledge… Faith.

An exciting and challenging ministry.

5.7 Crisis Pregnancy and Post Abortion Counselling

Janet Deavin describes a significant Church ministry which commenced in 2003 and continued for fifteen years:

"The doors of *Achor* opened in October 2003 to provide a safe place for women with an unintended pregnancy to talk through the issues facing them. One of the Elders of The

Coign Church, John Wardill, had the original vision for the Church to get involved in helping women who were considering abortion and also supporting those who had had an abortion. So a management team, led by Doreen Mellor, was established in December 2002 and *Achor Pregnancy Counselling Trust* was formed. The centre was named *Achor* - from Hosea Chapter 2 verse 15, "I will make the Valley of Achor (trouble) a door of hope" and our prayer was that Achor would be a door of hope to the women and men who came through it.

"The vision was to offer a caring compassionate non-judgmental counselling service without pressure to all women who were unintentionally pregnant or had a 'crisis' pregnancy so that they could make an informed choice concerning their pregnancy and also to support women who had been affected by abortion.

"We became affiliated to CARE Centres Network and obtained our training material as well as general support by means of education days and annual conferences from them. The first training course was held in 2003 and over the years several more were held. In total 35 people attended the training courses and 29 volunteers actually helped with *Achor*.

"Initially we used a room in the Woking Association of Voluntary Services building but when that was no longer available The Coign Church let us use one of the rooms in the *Acorn Centre* in Oaks Road and we moved there in January 2005. Then in 2008 we were also able to run two sessions a week in a room in the Contraception and Sexual Health (CASH) clinic in Woking Community Hospital which was an excellent location being right in the heart of family planning.

"It soon became apparent that there was also a need for support for those women who had had an abortion and so the team then trained as post abortion advisors.

"In 2007 Doreen stepped down from leading the team to concentrate on Evaluate, an education programme for schools. Presentations were given in 4 local schools, and were well received, but the schools were finding it hard to obtain the necessary funding for this and the work ended three years later. Janet took over the leading of the team assisted by Gill Gloster and Tina Maskell.

"In 2009 the team joined the CareConfidential helpline and covered two sessions a week on a national helpline for those with unintended pregnancy and post abortion questions. And in 2011, Gill Gloster who had always had a heart for working with women in prison, joined the Chaplaincy team at HMP Send to support women with child loss of various kinds, mostly compulsory adoption. Gill now concentrates almost exclusively on this area and has spent time with more than 30 women prisoners over the last five years.

"Over the years the crisis pregnancy scene changed, and crisis pregnancy centres were coming under keen scrutiny from outside agencies. With this in mind CareConfidential separated from CARE in 2012 in order not to be associated with a campaigning organisation, as the need for non-biased counselling and advice was seen as paramount.

"By 2016 it was felt that the crisis pregnancy work of Achor was no longer viable, this was due to a number of reasons namely:- a significant drop in women seeking advice, (this was also reflected in the other centres in the UK) largely due to the increasing popularity of the medical abortion (i.e. taking two pills) and the necessity to do this before 9 weeks, the increasing need to provide a more professional level of counselling that was not feasible with volunteers who were only seeing a client once every few months, and the fact that most of the volunteers were unable to continue with the work. At the same time CareConfidential also folded. So I (Janet) continued with just the post abortion work and Gill continued to work with women in prison.

"Over the period of 15 years Achor helped nearly 450 women, including those in prison, more than 100 of which were for support following an abortion or child loss, they had over 1300 contacts with clients including 300 in prison as well as answering over 800 calls on the CareConfidential helpline.

"In 2017 a new initiative was undertaken to deliver the 'Restore and Rebuild' course to Christian women with the emphasis on helping women from within the Church to resolve the issue of past abortion within the context of their faith and to see healing in their lives in this area".

CHAPTER 6

FURTHER MEMORIES

6.1 Families' camps

One of the most popular and keenly awaited events on the Church calendar between 1966 and 1974 were the yearly Church families' camps. Ron Newman, Alan Sussex, Eddie Bower and David Dennington initially put pen to paper and the following is a composite description of events.

The purpose of these holidays was for fellowship, fun and teaching. In turn they became places where lasting friendships were made across the generations which have stood the test of time.

Initially families' camps were held at Swanage, Dorset near where the Durlston Country Park is currently situated. In 1971 the venue moved from Swanage to Charmouth, also in Dorset. Each year around 100 Church members and families packed their camping belongings, said farewell to commuting or town life in Woking and set out for a primitive week by the sea. Great fun!

A Camp Commandant was responsible for the practical day to day running of the camp and a Padre/Chaplain, the spiritual. It was at one of these camps in 1972 that a young Terry Virgo who was based at Seaford, Sussex and later became the Leader of New Frontiers International for many years, acted as Camp Chaplain.

Each morning at Swanage the children marched or ran off to have their own service overlooking the lighthouse. For the adults it was a more sedate awakening which started with morning cups of tea delivered to the tent doors.

Shudders came upon Eddie (and probably many more) when he recalled from his distant past "Those army tents we all used and latrines that the men had to dig, drying nappies in the cooking tent, primitive times, seeing each other first thing in the morning certainly broke down barriers, especially when you were on early morning tea duties, delivering to hands and bleary faces."

All of the families ate together in a big marquee. The food was prepared and cooked by willing volunteers who had to get up early in the morning, miss morning trips away from the campsite, then prepare lunch and yes, you have got it right, get ready for the evening meal. Just to make certain that the cooks had a good night's sleep cocoa was served last thing (doesn't sound like a holiday to me).

The evening services were led by the Chaplain and produced many exciting times of worship and teaching. At one camp George Tarleton introduced the subject of praying for healing. He asked if anyone had a bad back. A dozen or so campers came forward. Then he sat down on the floor in front of them and lifted their legs to examine if one was shorter than the other (a common cause of many back problems). Then he prayed for God to come and adjust the length. David Dennington recalls George Tarleton praying for Derrick Ball, an Elder and a man of great faith. "As he prayed Derrick`s leg grew so much that it had to be prayed back. I actually saw it grow. It is a common practice now but to see a leg grow was an amazing revelation of God`s Power."

One of the highlights remembered by many was "Hunt the Parent" throughout the local town. The game was simple: parents disguised themselves and the children had to find them. If they thought that they had recognised an adult the children had to ask, "Do you wear long socks in bed at night?" The game was not that simple as the parents dressed up in various forms of disguise and found various nooks and crannies around the town of Swanage. The following characters were seen wandering around the streets:

- A gentleman in white coat and clerical collar posing as a local Vicar (Bob Boorman)
- Another in dark overalls manning the pumps at a local garage (Alan Sussex)
- Two more posing as pop singers in flared trousers with long haired wigs and hair bands (David Dennington and Peter Lander)

- Yet another kitted out in a long brown mackintosh and dark beret posing as Frank Spencer looking for his "Betty"
- A French onion seller complete with beret and bicycle (Chas Davis)
- An apparently heavily pregnant lady endeavouring to walk across a zebra crossing (Margaret Askew, who recalls crossing the road more times that afternoon than she can remember)
- A heavily intoxicated woman armed with a bottle slumped outside the local pub (Alice Potter dressed in her husband's clothes) *[Editor's note: I'm not surprised that her daughters failed to recognise her]*

One night at Charmouth, because of a scare of intruders, a guard patrolled the area walking around the camp, stopping at each tent and praying for each person inside.

Who could forget the last night's sing song round the camp fire, featuring such artists as David Field singing, "You push the damper in and you pull the damper out and the smoke goes up the chimney just the same" and Len Chart leading more singing with the finale camp song in which all the happenings of the week were put to song (Andrew Lloyd Webber eat your heart out). For the brave the holiday ended with a midnight swim followed by bubble and squeak in the cookhouse.

6.2 Women's meetings

Olive Davis records her involvement in the running of special weekly meetings for the women of the Church:

"In 1953 Chas and I together with our daughter Gwen moved from London to the new estate at Sheerwater. As Chas was doing National Service we did not transfer our membership from Rye Lane Baptist Church until he was demobbed and we could be part of Woking Baptist Church as a family.

"In the early 1950s Margaret Askew and I were invited to attend the Women's meeting with our babies, Bobby and Gwen, in their prams, who we left at the back of the Hall. The meeting was run by the pastor's wife, Mrs Fraser, (Rev

Leslie Frazer preceded Philip Jones) assisted by the deacon's wives (all wearing hats, of course).

"Some years later Mary Child took over the leadership and changed the name of the meeting to Welcome Hour, where ladies sat in a circle around a coffee table. We sang hymns, read the Bible and prayed. One day Ted Appleton called in to pay for his wife's Bible notes "Every Day with Jesus". Mary invited him to stay to the meeting and he kept coming regularly. During the years that followed there were always a few men among the ladies.

"Mary Child moved away because of her husband's job, so as I attended with my Mum I was asked to take over the leadership. Reluctantly I agreed to take on the role for a year - and stayed on for nearly 35 years, until 2008 when Malcolm and Fran Surman took over with a team and *Options* started, for the over 60s, with lunches and coffee mornings, Art and Skittles, Walks, Bible Studies, Gardener's Club, Hymn Singing, Craft Activity Groups, visits to Theatre and Cinema, Golf, Table Tennis and Bird Watching. These were designed to for all over 60s including those who may not attend The Coign."

6.3 Read all About it!

Chas Davis remembers the weekly information sheet:

"I was browsing recently, through some old copies of the Woking Baptist Church magazines of the 1960's, 1961 to 1968 to be precise. I saw that in October 1961, I was asked to take over the editorship of the then **Newsletter**, as it was called. It was fascinating to see how things had changed. Almost everyone was called by their title of either Mr. Jones or Mrs. Smith or Miss Evans. Referring to people by their first names wasn't quite proper. Without being critical, it seemed to reflect the level of friendship or intimacy. However, things did eventually change during Harold Owen's time as our Pastor. It was also a time when everyone was into LSD, not the drug, but the currency of Pounds, Shillings and Pence, i.e. £ s. d. Those of you reading this and under the age of say 30 or 40 years of age, may not be too familiar with the description of the currency then!

"It was the time when computers (PCs) were in their infancy, mobile phones were perhaps as large as bricks, ipods we would have thought of as something to do with flying saucers. And 'blackberries' were definitely something you ate. One edition mentioned *TOP GEAR*. This was a coffee bar ministry with the Young People. So, TOP GEAR, you saw it first in the early period of the Woking Baptist Church. (Jeremy Clarkson, eat your heart out.) Another issue referred to a family in the church named Buckler, Bill and Peggy. Some may still remember them. They had a son named Paul Richard Buckler. You must have heard of the pop group called The Jam. Well, Paul Richard Buckler, better known as Rick Buckler, was the drummer of The Jam". [*Editor's note*: *Alice Potter's claim to fame was that she taught him to play the pinano]*

6.4 The Boys' Brigade

David Field describes the Church's Boys' Brigade activities:

"The heyday of the Boys' Brigade (BB), with its semi-military guise, was in the 1930s and the early post war years. The great changes in society that began in the late fifties soon became a challenge to church based youth organizations. The ethos of BB with its emphasis on discipline, loyalty and attendance at a weekly Bible Class was in marked contrast to the anything goes mood of the "swinging sixties". Boys became aware of other attractions that made less demands. Changes in education were also a factor: senior boys in particular had to contend with the pressure of passing exams. Also, schools were able to provide facilities of a high standard for a variety of extracurricular activities.

"However, well established BB companies with well-planned programs and strong leadership continued to attract and hold boys if high standards were maintained. Generally, it was the large/medium sized companies that flourished whilst smaller companies with fewer resources faded.

"The 3rd Woking Company was formed at Percy Street Baptist Church in 1964 with Life Boys for younger boys. The leaders included Peter Lodge, Jack Welch, Ken Lund and Brian and Pat Checksfield. In 1967 Brian Bonnington, having led a company in Sheerwater, was appointed Captain. The hard work put in by the leaders in the early days to establish the company brought rewards later as the company grew in numbers, achieved success in various competitions, produced annual displays of a good standard and enjoyed splendid summer camps in Croyde Bay, Swanage and other southern resorts. During this period I (David) joined the staff and became Captain in 1972. Other leaders played their part including Kath Pageot, Dennis & Sandra White, Bob King, Peter Smith and Richard Gardiner.

"When the BB was founded in 1883 its object was declared to be 'The Advancement of God's Kingdom among Boys'. The broader aims were to help boys to become men of character and integrity and train them in leadership. To what extent was this achieved in the Woking Company? One answer can be seen in the number of men, now middle aged, who serve in our Church or in other Churches: to their number should be added the men in The Coign who were once in the BB in other companies. In addition to happy memories of BB activities and camps these men testify to the part the BB played in their coming to faith in Jesus and preparing them for life's challenging demands."

6.5 Oh What a Sweetie!

Ron Newman records the weekly activity of one special Church member:

"One of my lasting memories of life at Percy Street in the 1960s was the "sweetie man". I have no idea why Gilbert Simmonds, or Mr. Simmonds as he was known, a much loved and respected Church Elder and Missionary Secretary always turned up for a Sunday morning service at Percy Street with a large bag of sweets. I guess it was his way of encouraging Church attendance. He could always be found in the entrance porch of the Church. Looking back, I wonder just how many elderly people or visitors were knocked over in the stampede to get to Gilbert. Whatever the number thanks to Gilbert for providing some very welcome sweets. How about restarting it today, but this time only for those over sixty?

"In 1968 when Gilbert was becoming fairly advanced in years he passed over the responsibility of being the sweet monitor to me. Each week Gilbert would pass me a large bag of Mackintosh Quality Street and at the end of the morning service I would stand outside, and all the children were allowed to take one sweet each. Despite requests from those of more advanced years there was a strictly ‘no adult’ rule.”

6.6 The Coign Goes to Pot

Geoff Owers recounts an unexpected and humorous event which occurred some years ago in relation to the garden outside of the kitchen as you approach the entrance to The Coign.

“For some years I tended this strip of land with spring and summer displays. Apart from fighting nature with all its elements, not to mention the weeds, there was always a variety of cigarette ends to clear away.

One day I noticed something different – it looked like a respectable plant, but as I wasn’t sure what it was I decided to leave it. When it got to two or three feet high some of The Coign members who were more knowledgeable than me suggested that perhaps it should be removed before we became a feature in the local news and possibly taken to court. It was a cannabis plant!”

6.7 Purest of Motives

Heather Britt (nee Jones, Philip Jones' daughter) - a memory of hers:

"One of my memories as a teenager at Percy Street is of Boys' Club Camp... as a sixteen-year-old girl I'm sure I must have had the purest of motives for going along to help with the camp cooking! The Boys' Club was run by Mr Frank Payne and I think his wife Mary was probably in charge of the cooking. I remember Jenny Brooksbank (Gloster), and I think Linda Payne also came along to help. The camp was at Hastings and I can picture the cliff-top camp site, but the strangest part of the whole thing was our mode of transport to and from Hastings; we travelled in the back of a furniture van, no doubt perched on tent packs, boxes of provisions etc! Health and Safety regulations?... there probably weren't any, but we were all safe, extremely healthy and we had a great time!!"

6.8 Youth Weekends

Young Peoples' Youth Weekends at Ventnor on the Isle of Wight played an important part in my spiritual awakening.

John Gloster

I, John Gloster, remember the excitement of the train and ferry journeys, St Rhadagunds as the venue and many of the walks and visits to Ventnor and other parts of the island including Blackgang Chine. They took place over a long weekend in half term and on the Sunday evening we would visit the little Baptist Chapel in Niton, a few miles away. It was at this service that the Bible teaching of the whole weekend came to a climax in a challenge to respond to the gospel message. It was an emotional event which influenced the direction of my life up until this day.

6.9 Chaplaincies

David Dennington records the Church's involvement with several outside organisations:

"During Harold's time the leaders became honorary chaplains to the British Airways Christian union at Heathrow for both male and female stewards. We would be asked to speak in the St. George's Chapel in Terminal 2. Stories of healing and deliverance, invitations to weddings and more.

The Aldershot and Pirbright army chaplains came as a group with some of the army lads. We had the privilege of leading one of the chaplains to Christ. Harold refused to baptise him for a year or more, but in the end as he insisted, he was baptised. As a result, he was excommunicated by his church, that then led to him having his army commission withdrawn and losing his job. His family were in married quarters, so they lost their home. His children were in boarding school paid for by the army, so the school refused their places. He eventually became a Baptist pastor of a church in Scotland.

St Peters Hospital Christian Union became closely linked to the Percy Street Church and eventually Brian and Pat Checksfield took them into the central group and later they became a home group in Chertsey. This, of course, brought a lovely range of nationalities and eventually interesting weddings".

CHAPTER 7

CHURCH BUILDINGS

7.1 Suddenly… it Was All So Simple

Along with growth through evangelism, other Christians joined the Church, swelling Church membership to around 220 in 1968. This presented its own challenges. Simply the premises in Percy Street, which had remained unaltered for forty years, were not big enough or suitable to meet the needs of the Church. A number of plans were forthcoming, and included building a modern kitchen, toilet, meeting room, replacing the Young People's coffee bar, building a purpose-built recording studio and modernising the two cottages next to the Church. Following discussions with the Planning Department of Woking Borough Council it was decided at that time to proceed with the kitchen build. In 1969 plans were drawn up to replace the two cottages with a larger structure. Woking Borough Council was not minded to grant approval for this venture. Plans and modifications went through many stages until 30 October 1970 when the local planning committee approved the overall site development depending on a final decision from North West Surrey Planning Committee. This approval was not forthcoming. Another option emerged – It was suggested that the Church could sell the whole site to a developer and build a new building on an alternative location near the centre of Woking. In 1972 it was decided to explore this option further. Following the placement of an advert for interested property developers, twenty-eight tenders were received ranging from £290,000 to £401,000. At the same time negotiations were in progress for purchasing a number of properties in Oaks Road and some on the corner of Church Street. Then the bank interest rate suddenly increased and this in turn lead to a national economic crisis. The overall result was that property developers withdrew their offers, the Church had purchased seven properties and was some £60,000 in debt. Despite faithful giving by the members (some £15,000) this had risen to £66,833 by January 1975.

The financial situation became worse over the coming months, coming to a head one Sunday in March 1975. Instead of a normal Sunday sermon, the Pastor outlined the Church's financial situation. The Church had a massive bridging loan which was attracting monthly bank charges. At that date the debt stood at £80,000. Whilst members had generously contributed money to resolve the shortfall, the capital was not being reduced; in fact it was still growing. Members were asked to think and pray concerning how to reduce the debt. Harold Owen announced that there would be a 'giving morning' in seven days' time. After communion on the following Sunday, members each gave as they felt able. Geoff Owers, the Church Treasurer records the event:

"Row by row and one by one members left their seats and went forward. It was a massive offering to count. Brian Bonnington, I and two members of our families spent an hour counting the money". By lunchtime £42,000 had been given or promised. There were no specific large gifts, and nothing was contributed from the other Church funds; rather, everybody gave something; some sold their cars, others jewellery, cameras, others gave cash and some IOUs. Overall this worked out as an average of £120 per member. This was an amazing Sunday and never to be forgotten by those who attended - it became known as 'Mountain Sunday'. Whilst all were amazed, some were a little disappointed as they had believed that God would provide the full amount. God had other plans. He had taught members a lesson on giving and this resulted in the unlocking of people's hearts and money over the coming months.

"The news of 'Mountain Sunday' spread through the local press and even formed part of an article in the Readers Digest Magazine. The article was headlined 'Hallelujah Christians?' (January 1997) 'Charismatics point to many examples where the revival – they call it the "new wine" of the Spirit – has motivated whole congregations. Eighteen months ago Woking Baptist Church had a building debt of £80,000. "We felt the debt was dishonouring to God" says its Minister the Reverend Harold Owen, “so we had a ‘giving’ morning. People gave cheques, sold property, brought cameras, jewellery and valuables to the Communion table. We received £42,000 by lunchtime.” ’ ”

The need for larger, more suitable premises remained but the way forward was unclear. The Church owned both the Percy Street building and site and property in Goldsworth Road. The Church leadership were of the view that God would have to once again intervene. This God did, and only months later a property developer offered to design and build free of charge a purpose-built church building on the land owned by the Church in Church Street/Oaks Road in exchange for the property and land in Percy Street. This offer was gladly accepted, and events started to happen very quickly. All the required planning permissions were obtained, and it was agreed that the first stage of the work would be to demolish the building in Percy Street. The last service was held in Percy Street on 31st December 1976. The Church was faced with the prospect of having nowhere to meet whilst the building work took place. A temporary home for the congregation was offered by two local churches. Sunday afternoon services were held, with the kind permission of Rev Bishop, at Trinity Methodist Church in Brewery Road and other activities at St Mary of Bethany Church in York Road.

The new Church premises, were opened on 8 October 1977 with Nellie Hicks, one of the longest serving members, formally handing over the keys of the new building to the Pastor. It originally seated three hundred and fifty in the Chapel, one hundred in the Hall plus a further one hundred and fifty in a coffee lounge area, (Subsequently, of course, the seating capacity in the Chapel has been reduced somewhat, first with the creation of the “musicians’ corner” and later with the addition of the sound desk.

The building was named “The Coign”, which is an old English word meaning cornerstone or vantage point. A strange name, but how did it come about? Olive Davis recalls a conversation she had with Harold:

“Over the years Harold had emphasised that the Church is the 'people of God' and not the church building, so he wanted some suggestions for a suitable name for the new building. A variety of names were suggested and rejected. So I settled down in my bedroom to pray and ask God for a suitable name and as I prayed I remembered that Alan and Beryl Sussex lived in a house in Horsell and on a corner, called The Coign, meaning a 'Corner' or 'Cornerstone'. So, I rang Harold and reminded him of this and he responded, 'That's it; that's the name we want.' "

A brief service of dedication followed and in excess of one thousand cups of tea were served to visitors during the day. The opening day closed with a service of praise.

In the Church Secretary's report at the Annual Church meeting it is recorded that "After nine years of effort, worry and frustration suddenly the Lord moved, and it was all so simple. The last residue of the debt was paid. The money, Woking Borough Council planning, the actual building, clearing of the old building, where to go whilst we were without a building, what to do without a vestry…. there are no problems in Heaven, only plans". In the previous year (1975) the Church had an overdraft of £67,000, but by 1 January 1976 this had reduced to

£19,000. The debt had been completely eliminated by the time we left Percy Street at the end of December

The rest of the chapter is based heavily on text supplied by Mike Deavin

7.2 We need a bigger building

"We need a bigger building", this comment has been made at many Church meetings over the years and could easily have been relevant in the 1990s, 2000s and 2010s. But it was first made in January 1980; just two and a half years after the new building for The Coign Church had been opened. The minutes of a Church meeting in January 1980 said; "The shortage of sufficient space on Sundays and mid-week is becoming a major issue. In particular there is a shortage of counselling rooms on a Sunday evening, the lounge is too small and there is a need for a seminar room for meeting with other Church leaders".

The new home for The Coign Church was opened in October 1977 but within a couple of years there was insufficient space to accommodate the increase in numbers and the changes of uses within the building. In fact, within seven years of the new building opening, membership had almost doubled to 550 in 1985.

By early 1982 the Coign building had been extended with the construction of a new meeting room, utilising the area that was known as the 'Walled Garden', and a large study and office had been completed. The cost of this building work was in excess of £50,000 and some of the finance was raised through a special gift day which raised over £10,000.

7.2.1 Congregations Arrive

By late 1980, consideration was already being given to splitting into more than one congregation for Sunday morning meetings and although the extension in 1982 did provide additional facilities there was still insufficient space to accommodate all those who attended on a Sunday morning. As a result in April 1982 the Elders took the decision to create the first Sunday morning congregation in Horsell, at Sythwood School, and the Sunday evening meeting at The Coign took the form of a celebration. Less than a year later a second congregation was established in Knaphill.

By March 1985 there were a total of five congregations meeting to cater for the rapidly increasing membership. By 1986 a South Woking congregation was established making six congregations in total.

This split into congregations managed the lack of space for Sunday mornings, and attendance on a Sunday evening was always less than the mornings. As a result the Church suffered from not meeting all together; so in January 1991, shortly after the new leader, Malcolm Kayes, was appointed, the Church was brought back together with the Sunday morning meetings moved to Woking High School, where the main hall held 550 and there were excellent facilities for children's work.

7.2.2 The Focus on New Premises Increases

In 1991 Malcolm Kayes asked Mike Deavin, Chairman of the Trustees, to support the Church by heading up a team to investigate options for new premises; Mike worked in the construction industry for a national contractor and had been a Church member for 12 years. Mike recounts the long drawn out task of providing suitable accommodation to meet the needs of the on-going work of the Church.

"Around this time Woking Borough Council had drawn up plans for a canal-side marina which was to be located on the land from the canal up to Goldsworth Road with Oaks Road forming the western boundary. The Church entered into dialogue with WBC to explore the possibility of including a new extended church into the scheme or even selling the existing site to WBC and relocating elsewhere within the borough. The Council even explored the possibility of the church building being used as a 'Museum for Woking'.

"Alternative sites were few and far between, but St. Peter's Convent on Maybury Hill had become available and a feasibility study was carried out to establish whether a workable scheme should be progressed. Unfortunately, WBC did not have sufficient funds for the 'marina' scheme and St. Peter's Convent was found not to be suitable for our needs."

In July 1992 Mike Deavin led a group which was given the title the 'Nehemiah Task Force' to look at all the available options. In summary the report concluded that one (or more) of the following should be explored:

- Demolish the existing building and build larger premises on the site.
- Remodel and extend our current building.
- Sell our current site and construct a purpose made building on a new site.
- Enter into a Joint Venture with a contractor/developer to review options on our current site.
- Sell our current site and enter into a long-term lease for suitable premises.
- Investigate the possibility of increasing the size of our current site.

7.2.3 Our site expands

In early 1994 a unique opportunity presented itself to us. Sainsbury's had over the years purchased a number of the properties along Oaks Road; their plan was to construct a supermarket on the site. For a variety of reasons those plans were scrapped, and Sainsbury's wanted to sell five houses, all of them close to our site. An offer of £210,000 was accepted, a gift day was held within two weeks and the majority of funds required were raised on one Sunday morning, with the balance following soon after.

Most of the properties were in a very poor state of repair, some were even inhabited by squatters. A working party refurbished the buildings, and some were used for renting out whilst the others, following the award of a 'Temporary Change of Use' by Woking Borough Council, were converted to accommodate children's work and staff offices. These new buildings were named 'The Acorn Centre'. Following the completion of the work on the newly acquired properties it was decided to stop meeting at Woking Sixth Form College and hold two morning meetings at the Coign building, with children's work now being accommodated in 'The Acorn Centre'; this commenced in October 1994.

For the acquired site to be really useful we needed an entire area and unfortunately, one of the houses purchased, number 23, was remote for our site. However, one of our

Church members lived in number 19 and a swap, which was beneficial to both parties, was completed. These transactions significantly increased the area of our site but unfortunately two other properties still prevented us from owning an uninterrupted area, so the team stepped up efforts to purchase numbers seven and eleven Oaks Road. It was not until 2002 that both houses were finally purchased. The transaction to secure number eleven in 1997, was relatively straightforward but the saga involving the purchase of number seven (which had effectively become a 'ransom strip' on our site) would fill a book of its own!

7.2.4 The search for a new site continues

The team was now very aware of the value of our site and the search for a new site continued. With the help of local agents and a chartered surveyor we investigated over ten separate sites, making significant bids for many of them. Some of the sites are listed below:

- Lismore site at the corner of White Rose Lane and Heathside Road.

- Site on Goldsworth Park where the Salvation Army now have a building.
- Market Square as part of plans for redevelopment of the WBC scheme in 2002.
- A site behind the Holiday Inn Hotel on Church Street East.
- An industrial building on the Sheerwater Estate.
- Egley Road – now the site of a new school.
- A site at the top of Poole Road
- The site of the old Goldsworth Arms in Goldsworth Road

All of the above were reviewed and considered, some were rejected for a variety of reasons, and for some we submitted a bid after consultation with our advisors, but none of them came to fruition.

The reality was that it was almost impossible for The Coign Church to compete in the property market, the costs of sites escalated rapidly as residential developers got involved and we continually found ourselves out-bid by wealthy property developers. Woking Borough Council were always very supportive, except when, in 2000, we applied for planning permission on the Brewery Road car park site, which at the time was owned by the council. In hindsight it was probably not our wisest move but ironically, this move brought us to the attention of the council, and particularly Ray Morgan, the Chief Executive, who politely explained to us the error of our ways, and has since then steadfastly supported us with ideas, other options and in some cases design input.

7.2.5 A change of direction - upwards

In 2005 the building team decided to take a different approach and invited Warings, a Portsmouth-based construction company where Mike Deavin was Construction Director, to undertake a review of what options might be available to us.

The Business Development department at Warings took up the challenge with enthusiasm and quickly formed a Joint Venture with a developer called Friday Street, based in Odiham. The newly formed JV company was aptly named

Cornerstone and they worked on a scheme which focussed on maximising the value of our entire site.

It was at this time that the Trustees felt that is was important to seek professional support to steer us through the next phase of our development, and after a thorough review of a number of local Project Managers, Michael Edwards Associates (MEA) from Eashing were appointed. Mike O'Hanlon, the principal director, was soon to become an integral part of our team going forwards.

Also, around this time the officers at Woking Borough Council were grappling with the issue of meeting their required quota of housing units that had been set by central government, whilst at the same time protecting the 'Green Belt' which surrounded the Borough – the only real way was up, and that had to be in the town centre.

With the above in mind and, encouraged by some members from the local authority, Cornerstone quickly came up with a proposal which included two large tower blocks housing 180 flats for retail and a 1,000-seater church with associated facilities at 'cost neutral', meaning that the Church would pay nothing. The Elders and the Trustees considered this proposal and decided to instruct Cornerstone to proceed to planning as this represented a very cost-effective solution to our long-term search for larger premises.

By late 2006 Cornerstone were close to submitting an application for planning permission and a Public Consultation was held. It is fair to say that some of our near neighbours were less than enamoured by our proposed new building and we managed to make the front page of the local paper. Unfortunately, just as our planning application was close to completion in late 2007, the economy took a nose dive, first Barings Bank then Northern Rock collapsed, and suddenly funding that was available to developers disappeared almost overnight and our scheme, along with many others across the country, was shelved.

The economic downturn lasted longer than anyone had feared, and despite working with MEA to come up with a variety of different proposals for our site none were felt to be viable, especially with the prospect of a new church at no cost still somewhere in the background.

7.2.6 Along came the French

It was during this economic downturn that Warings were purchased by the French company Bouygues, one of the largest construction conglomerates in the world, and within two years Bouygues opened a development company in the UK which focussed its attention on clients who had land and a scheme, but not the wherewithal to progress. Their business model was aimed at finding work and vital turnover for their construction companies.

In 2010 the team from Bouygues Development set about reviewing the design and entering into serious discussions with the Planning Department at Woking Borough Council on our behalf. Unfortunately, as time had passed it appeared that the desire for such high buildings had diminished and the past design had to be considerably scaled down. The end result, after a great deal of discussion and redesign, was a single, much smaller tower and only 85 residential units. The result of this was that the church building not only had to be reduced to seat 800, but there was also a funding gap to cover of around £1.5m. With no other options available at this time the Elders and Trustees considered that £1.5m was an acceptable price to pay for a building that would still meet our requirements.

After a lengthy pre-planning process, with yet more appearances in the local paper, our proposal was eventually granted planning consent in March 2015 by an overwhelming majority of the Planning Committee.

Sadly, the euphoria of the planning victory didn't last long. Bouygues were undergoing a change of personnel, replacing the longstanding team with those who had limited knowledge of the project. This new team, following the granting of the planning consent, undertook a detailed viability study and found that the project was no longer viable. At a meeting in June 2015, Bouygues Development announced their withdrawal from the scheme and the building team were, in effect, back to square one.

7.2.7 Other options explored

All was not lost. The Church had a scheme which had been designed as well as a planning consent; the challenge was now to find a developer who could help make it come to fruition. In the next twelve months discussions were held with Fizzy Living, the company who had been chosen by Bouygues to purchase the completed building. Fizzy Living were very keen on the scheme, Woking was an ideal place for their brand and they worked diligently to see if they could develop the scheme themselves. After about six months they decided that the company did not have the capacity for such a project.

Immediately after Fizzy Living had declined to proceed, Woking Borough Council approached the Church to use the site for much needed low-cost housing, which could not be accommodated in the Victoria Square scheme, which was at that time heading towards planning. The idea was to increase the size of the flats to suit families; this reduced the number of units and put further pressure on the size and facilities for our new church. The final design reduced the church building footprint to little more than we already had, so this option had to be declined.

One final attempt was made to get the scheme off the ground, when we approached a Housing Association who worked with a national contractor and were confident they could make the scheme work. A few months later we received the same message: unless the height of the tower could be increased by a few more storeys the scheme was not viable.

7.2.8 A new helmsman

In December 2012 Guy Miller, the leader of the Commission group of churches, gave a prophecy at a Sunday morning meeting; this later became known as 'The Barge Prophecy'. Guy saw a row of five locks on a canal and a barge progressing through them. Each lock represented a phase of the Church and although we didn't know it at the time, we were heading into that 4th lock.

"The 4th lock is like a refurb lock. It's time for a rubbing down, it's time for a name change, it's time for when things have to change, and paint has to be peeled off and a new lick of paint applied – to interact with the age with which this Church will interact. I see a new helmsman being ushered on board, I see the boat rising and rising"

A combined church and residential development project had been on the table for a twelve-year period and whilst there were periods of inaction during that time a great deal of effort had been invested in the scheme by many people. However, at a meeting between the Building Team and the Elders in March 2016 the difficult decision was taken to formally drop the proposal.

One of the major frustrations of all the iterations of the combined scheme was that the Church building team was never really in control. For understandable reasons, the organisation who was investing in the region of £25m wanted to call the shots, and our contribution of just over one million pounds meant that our ability to drive the project was stifled.

So, at the aforementioned meeting it was decided that The Coign Church would 'take control' and develop our own project on our own site.

At this time Malcolm Kayes, our leader of 27 years, decided that the timing was right for him to put down the leadership of The Coign Church. Malcolm was always totally committed to the previous project giving clear and focussed leadership along the way. He had always promised to see the project through had it gone ahead, as he felt that it would have been unfair to land a new leader with a large construction project where he had neither the vision nor the input.

Any new building project would now become the responsibility of our future leader, but things did not slow down for long. In January 2017 Steve Petch was appointed as the new leader of The Coign Church and would formally start with the church on 1st September 2017.

7.2.9 A new direction

Steve Petch was very keen to learn the history and the background of the building project and started the learning process well before his official start date with the Church, attending a number of meetings in the months leading up to his commencement.

Steve very quickly supported the principle of 'taking control' of our own development and in June 2017 produced a short paper. His summary makes interesting reading:

"The ultimate aim is a building, or buildings, that represent the Church well and provide for the meeting needs of The Coign Church - both on Sundays and during the week. We want a building that people in Woking will be aware of, and we should aim to give every person in the community of Woking a reason to come through the doors once a year: to vote … to attend an event or a conference … to take part in a community activity … to access a ministry of the Church and more."

The Building Team moved swiftly and produced a plan to ensure that no time was lost in moving towards the next phase of our eventful journey. The idea was to demolish the existing houses and build a standalone auditorium, or chapel, to the rear of the existing building which would seat around 650 people. The existing building would then be reconfigured to create a large entrance foyer and cater for our children's work. The building work would also include a remodelled kitchen and an extension at the front to house new staff offices.

By September 2017 Plan A were appointed as our architects for the scheme. Plan A quickly caught the vision of the team and produced a number of schemes which were whittled down to one which was acceptable to the team. A positive pre-planning application meeting was held with

Woking Borough Council in December 2017 and, after consultation with Church members and our neighbours in February 2018, planning application was submitted in April 2018. It is also important to note that our neighbours were much more receptive towards the new scheme, and the coverage of the local paper was far more positive too.

The finances for the new building presented the next challenge; there was no developer on board to cover the majority of our costs this time. The build costs for the new scheme were originally estimated to be in the order of £4m and the principle of securing a commercial mortgage for around half of those costs was agreed by the Trustees. Gift Days were held across three Sundays at the end of April and early May, 2018. The result was truly staggering as over £1.4m was given towards the new project. The general fund had a significant cash balance in anticipation of this project, so the costs of the new building were already almost met.

In July O&D Construction, a construction company from Godalming, was appointed as our preferred contractor to work with us on design and to agree a fixed price during the second stage of the tender process. The final costing meant that a further £600,000 would be needed together with the loan and previous giving. Two further Gift Days were held in November, 2018, to help defray the amount

The final hurdle, our planning application was heard by Woking Borough Council on 4 September 2018. It was approved!

The exciting story of all that happened next will be a tale to be told in another volume.

CHAPTER 8

A PASTOR'S VIEW

Malcolm Kayes writes:

I had the privilege and joy of leading The Coign Church from 1991 to 2017 but I started serving the church at the start of 1989 when I was still on staff and an elder at Bracknell Baptist Church. The Coign Fellowship had experienced a difficult leadership transition prior to 1989 and was increasingly becoming fractured and distracted, despite the good efforts of some of its leaders and Terry Virgo. The Coign had for many years been part of the Newfrontiers family of churches, of which Terry was the founder and leader, and he had been asked to help the Church recover and find a new leader.

Eventually Terry Virgo, with the agreement of most leaders, disbanded The Coign Eldership and asked one of those elders, Howard Dodge, to become caretaker leader. He also recommended that I started serving and strengthening the Church through occasional preaching and by meeting regularly with Staff and wider leadership, whilst he continued his search for a leader.

It was a painful and disturbing season for the Church – a group left to start another local church, there were some necessary staff changes, and now they had this 'northerner' getting involved. However, God's grace was on us all as we worked together and slowly started to recover, still waiting for Terry to identify and recommend the new leader. Several months later, I was asked by The Coign leaders to consider leaving Bracknell to lead The Coign Fellowship, but as we had just completed a 1000 seater church building in Bracknell the leaders there were unwilling to release me, and I was not looking for a move anyway, even though I really enjoyed being amongst the Coign folk who had shown great perseverance and joy despite their recent history.

It was in Autumn 1990, and no new leader had yet been found for The Coign Church when I was surprisingly 'loosened' from Bracknell and then through the invitation, guidance, and recommendation of Coign leaders and Terry Virgo, and the agreement of the Church members, I was appointed to lead the Church from January 1991.

The Coign Fellowship had mostly recovered from its pain and hurt at that time and though Howard, me and many others had sought to serve the people and ministries well in the waiting period, it still lacked clear leadership appointments and direction. So, with leadership authority and responsibility now clearly invested in me, I felt more freedom to bring much stronger cohesion and confidence to the people and ministries of the Church, and hopefully restore an Eldership. A year later, and there was an Eldership Team in place and in the next few years we changed the name from The Coign Fellowship to The Coign Church, adjusted some of our social action and midweek ministries, and started to make plans to return from using local schools and colleges to meet again on Sunday mornings at the Coign building.

I had also been asked by Terry Virgo to serve and support two other local Newfrontiers churches in Chertsey and Shepperton and this was progressing quite well. The Coign Church members were wonderful in accepting and accommodating my occasional trips out to these other churches and increasingly to churches overseas, in the Netherlands and India for example.

Several other Newfrontiers churches also sought my help, and other churches were being adopted into our Apostolic family. At the same time, the Elders reviewed several significant prophecies given previously to the church about being 'an Antioch Church' (Acts 11&13); a local church willing both to receive helpful ministry and to be generous in resourcing other churches and agencies in their mission. We decided, by the grace of God and with great reliance upon His strength, to be intentional in pursuing and enabling The Coign Church to be such an Antioch Church. Church members responded with such faith and energy to this vision and to our mission of 'meeting people's real needs with God's real power'. We appointed balanced staff teams that could both build up The Coign Church and serve other churches locally and internationally. Eventually, the

Church would become the hub for over twenty other Newfrontiers UK churches working together on mission and would have many fruitful connections with churches in over twenty nations.

One year, 1994, was exceptional in blessings, challenges, and change. The blessings came as we gave room for what was called 'The Toronto Blessing'. Emanating from Canada, this was a move of the Holy Spirit that refreshed and revived many in the Church. It was a very irreligious, noisy, and hilarious season for us as a Church. A few of the evident manifestations of the Spirit's presence might have been copycat actions, but the clear majority were genuine as God poured His love into our hearts by His Spirit. The challenges came as we were given an opportunity to purchase defunct Sainsbury-owned properties adjacent to the Coign building in Oaks Road. Acquiring these properties would enable us to return to hosting Sunday morning meetings at our own building. Again, Church members gave so willingly and generously in one offering, so we purchased the buildings and refurbished them. That was the first of many steps by which we eventually came to own a complete plot of land in Oaks Road. Change came in two forms that year. First as we moved towards holding two Sunday morning meetings back at The Coign, with our children being able to meet for part of that time in separate rooms in our newly acquired and refurbished Acorn Centre. The second significant change came as we stopped our familiar midweek house-group meetings and replaced them with single-sex discipleship groups for three or four persons. These discipleship groups continued successfully for several years and, I believe, built a strong biblical foundation in many lives. Many close and caring relationships that were developed in those small groups have stood the test of time.

Our Sunday meetings were always genuinely open to contributions from members of the congregation and, though this was messy at times, it was a key factor in the building up of the Church. I had several unchurched visitors ask me a similar question: 'How did you orchestrate that?' referring to individuals 'spontaneously' praying, reading a Bible verse, starting a song, prophesying, and testifying during our meetings. When I denied any orchestration or pre-planning they were incredulous, as they had heard and recognised a clear theme and flow as God encouraged and ministered to us by His Spirit and through His people exercising His gifts.

At one joint-church event a lady asked me which church I attended. When I replied 'The Coign Church' she waved her hands in the air and whooped several times! She wasn't reflecting delight, it was her derisive impression of our worship style, though I don't think she had ever attended any of our meetings. We never 'swung from the rafters' during our worship as was our reputation amongst some local churches – mainly because the rafters were just out of reach.

The incredulity of guests was also evident during wedding receptions when I would point out to some that the food had been prepared and was being served by Church members. 'Come off it!' was the sharp reply from a solicitor – she wouldn't believe me – such was the excellence of the food and drink, the presentation, and the table service.

On the mission-front the church was substantially involved in the sending and supporting of many Coign folk in planting and leading UK churches in Chertsey, Camberley,

Newquay, Nottingham, and Guildford, and in Austin (Texas, USA). The times when we sent and supported our Coign friends out on these and other church planting adventures were both painful and exciting. We were saying farewell to close friends and colleagues, yet the birth of new churches was something we could celebrate.

In 2008 we undertook a major transition from two Sunday morning meetings at The Coign and moved to hosting one Sunday morning meeting at the larger HG Wells Conference facility in the town centre. We continued to meet at the Coign building for our evening meetings, but we were lacking enough room for visitors and our developing Coign Kids Work at our morning meetings, hence the move. The following year we needed a second morning meeting to cater for increasing attendance and, with the consequent greater demands upon our Sunday serving teams, we encountered one of the toughest dilemmas we faced as Elders – to continue with our Sunday evening meeting or not? We decided to stop our regular Sunday evening meetings. Our evening meetings had served us well for decades, providing times of extended worship and ministry, and opportunity to witness many baptisms and receive guest speakers. It would be hard to forget visits by Wimber teams, Ram Babu, and Jonathan Aitken (among many others), and the evening presentations of 'Heaven's Gates and Hell's Flames' were spectacular and fruitful with many responding to the gospel challenge.

I thank God for all of the fellow Elders and staff colleagues I worked alongside, and the hundreds of 'living stones' (1 Peter 2:5) that God has provided, added, and used in the building of The Coign Church over these past three decades – people who were alive in the Spirit and totally dependable – Jesus can build His church with such people and they helped me thoroughly enjoy my season leading The Coign Church. It was never a burden (Hebrews 13:17). Finally, to paraphrase Hebrews 11:32: And what more shall I say? I do not have time to tell about Howard, Alice, Brian, Andrew, Hazel, John, Maggie, Paul, Barry, Pam, Nick, Vera, Kim, Charlotte, Alan, Eleanor, Ron, Olive, Geoff, Mike, Mark, Karen, Gill, Les, David, Phil and the many, many other Coign folks who can be commended for their faith and service.

CHAPTER 9

CONCLUDING COMMENTS

Hopefully you have enjoyed reading this book, which has described some of the events which have shaped today's Welcome Church. Personally, to relive some of the past events and learn about others for the first time has been exciting, informative and above all a real privilege.

In Chapter 1 six reasons for writing the book were given. If I had to pick just one it would be to echo the words of the psalmist, David where he says "Great is the Lord and most worthy of praise; His greatness no-one can fathom. One generation will commend your works to another, they will tell of Your mighty acts."

God has been working in and through our local Church since its beginning in 1879 and will continue to do so. Whether it be in the construction and use of our new Church building or any other way He chooses, the story is still ongoing. In times to come one of our current young people will, no doubt, become inspired in later life to record it all, to pass on to future generations, too.

READ ALL THREE COMPANION VOLUMES

Church on the Move, Welcome Church Story

and *Living History*

by John Gloster

Church on the Move traces the history of the Baptist Church in Woking from its first meeting in 1879 when 40 gathered in a villa on Goldsworth Road, through to over 500 filling The Coign and looking for larger premises in 1999. The meticulously kept minutes of Church meetings over the years reveal the loving hand of God leading His Church through times of challenge and times of blessing to become a Christian community meeting people's real needs with God's real power.

Welcome Church Story majors on the years since the Church moved to The Coign – now The Welcome Centre – and gives a fuller account of how God has led His people through times of trial, miraculous provisions and light-hearted fun, calling upon the recollections of individuals in the Church at those times.

Living History focusses on specific areas of Welcome Church life such as the role of the trustees, personal stories of missionaries who travelled overseas, local outreach and Welcome Works that serve the community, the HG Wells Conference Centre years, Steve Petch's journey to Woking to become the new Lead Elder, the completion of the building project, the year in Lockdown, and personal testimonies of God's life-changing power.

Together, the three volumes provide a fascinating and inspiring account of God at work throughout 140 years of this Church's history, from small beginnings to a community of well over 700 men, women and children connected to Welcome Church in 2021—and the hundreds more in six church plants around the country and in the USA—impacting Woking and far beyond with the love of Jesus and the power of His Gospel.

All three books are available on Amazon and from John Gloster through Welcome Church at:

info@welcomechurch.uk

Made in the USA
Middletown, DE
28 December 2022

20445152R00087